GW00646702

Crochet

Two Continents Publishing Group

Crochet

Contents

Printed in The Netherlands

Two Continents
30 East 42 Street
New York, New York 10017

Library of Congress Cataloging in Publication Data

Klip, Rite van der.
Crochet.

Translation of Haken.
1. Crochet. 2. Soft sculpture. I. Title.
TT820.K69213 1977 746.4'34 76-52781

ISBN 0 8467 0240 1

Introduction

There is a place for some form of crochet work almost everywhere in your home, although many people do not realize this and, now that crochet is so popular, are limiting their work to clothing – hats, sweaters, baby clothes, and similar garments – despite the fact that the different techniques of crochet and the many different yarns for it almost demand something more than the traditional pot holder.

This book is designed to help you create crochet designs for your home. There are many patterns, clearly written, and most of the illustrated designs have suggestions with them so you can use your own ideas and imagination in your work.

Materials and colors are very important in your home and help in determining the atmosphere of it. For this reason, there are discussions of both colors and yarns and threads.

The beginner need not be afraid of this book. All the basic stitches are shown in the back of the book. Never start with a complicated pattern, but instead make a sampler using as many stitches and variations as possible. Keep such a sampler as a cherished possession as there may come a time when you will be looking for stitch ideas and your sampler will prove a source of inspiration.

Once you are able to crochet fairly well you can turn your attention to true works of art in three dimensions. A discussion of this area of crochet is found in the chapter on Free Crochet. Free crochet involves trying out your ideas, searching for good shapes and colors, and letting your imagination have free rein. This type of work will give you a tremendous feeling of satisfaction, as will working the other ideas in this book.

Rite van der Klip

1 Window Decoration

Windows are the eyes of a house. You look through them both out and in. Ordinarily the view is somewhat blocked by curtains, but there are many people who are tired of conventional curtains or draperies and want something else. Decorative crochet is one excellent solution. In this chapter you will find a number of suggestions and patterns so that you can crochet window coverings of the kind you want. It is, of course, important to take into consideration the function of the window you will decorate and the view through it of the outside world.

The Window

If the house is set back from the sidewalk there is less of a problem with people looking in than there is with a house or apartment that fronts directly onto the sidewalk.
The placement of the window from the point of view of light, that is, whether it gets sun or no sun, also plays an important role in deciding how it should be decorated.

No view in, no sunlight
This type of window is ideal for plants. Put plants on the window sill and hang plants from the top of the window frame and the window is 'dressed'. Plants are able to give a room something of the feeling of a greenhouse. We will start by making a crocheted net in which to hang an ornamental pot holding a plant. Choose a crochet yarn that takes color well, such as 100% cotton, since a dark window benefits from such colors as orange, yellow, purple, or red. You can, of course, choose to echo the colors of your draperies, if you have draperies. A net for a pot to hang in is simple to crochet; if you run into difficulties check the stitch glossary on page 85 and the picture on the next page.

Nets for Hanging Plants
Start with the bottom and crochet a chain of 8 stitches. Close this into a ring with a slip stitch. Crochet 6 times (8 loops and 1 single crochet) in this ring. In the following row crochet in every loop of chains 2 chain loops of 8 chains and 1 single crochet. This way there are 2 single crochets in every chain loop so that at the end of the row there are 16 such loops. If the flower pot is very large then you can continue this technique in the following row. Once the bottom is finished continue to crochet in chain loops until the right height for the pot is reached. Finish off. To hang the pot, crochet, using a double yarn, a long chain of loops, 6 times the length needed to hang the pot at the height you want it. Sew this cord through the top round of the holder and sew its beginning and its ending together. Put 3 loops on the net at the same distance apart and add a metal ring for hanging up the pot.

Window Hangings
If the design of your window is such that no plants can be hung in it then crocheted window hangings can be extremely attractive. These thread designs are made in various forms including round, square, and

A. Make the chain of stitches into a ring.

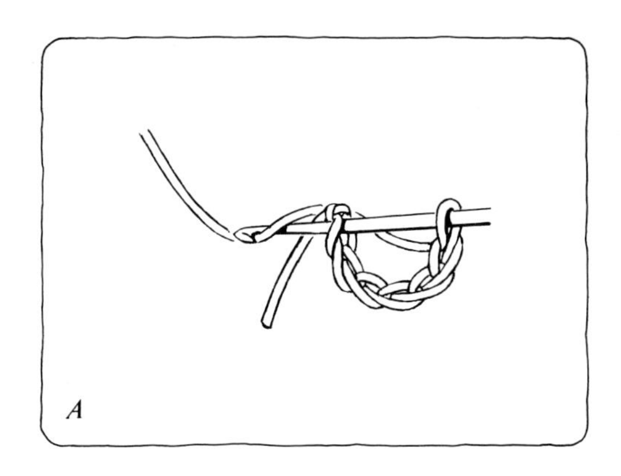

B. Crochet arches in the ring and in the following rows arches in arches.

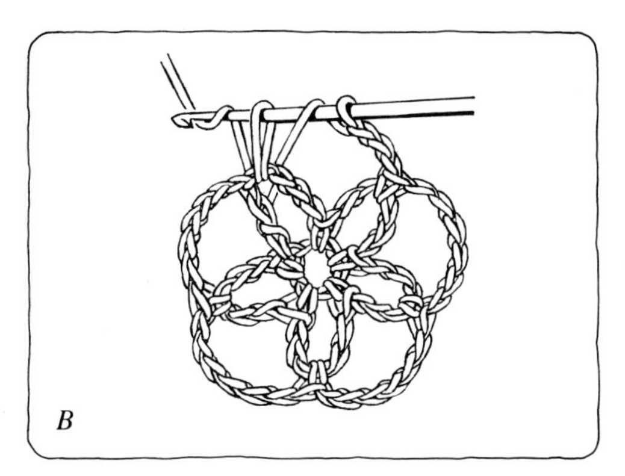

rectangular. On page 13 you can see an example of this type of decoration. If, for instance, the window is high and narrow, it might look better with 3 rings of different sizes hung one above the other.

No View in with Sunlight

The top of the window can be decorated with window hangings as described above. The colors used for these should either be related to your interior or be white. Various shades of green can be very effective in creating an outdoor feeling.

Screens can be made to protect the plants on the window sill against too much sun. You can use a *screen* if you want, removing the netting and making a piece of crochet to replace it. Filet crochet is excellent if it is worked with a thin crochet yarn, see filet crochet on page 10. It is a simple form of crochet made up of double crochet and chain stitches. If you are more skilled, you can make a piece of filet crochet into a truly dramatic work. Keep the crochet work fine so that its function as a screen is not lost.

Use quiet colors, for example white, ecru, green, or brown.

The Exposed Window

Some new houses have a large window by the front door or a large window in the front door itself that can make you feel you have no privacy.

If you don't want to have every Tom, Dick, and Harry looking in but do want to let the light in, the solution is a hanging curtain with stripes of solid fabric. This is not difficult to make.

This can also be used for other windows, such as a picture window or the bottom half of a window in the living room.

Hanging Curtains

Such a hanging curtain can be crocheted from the bottom and top in filet crochet work. The crocheted sections are joined with a crocheted chain decorated with a picot edge. These picots can be replaced with beads; see page 45. The stripe section stands out from the thickness of the beads.

The material for a hanging curtain depends upon the size of the window. If it is a high, wide window, then use a rougher thread or yarn than you would for a low, narrow window. Use threads that are colorfast and completely washable. Cotton is usually preferred for this reason. Don't use wool. Synthetic yarns, such as the ones developed for making sweaters, can be used double if you want.

The color will also play a part in helping you decide what yarn or thread you will use for your curtains. This must blend with the color of the door as well as the room or hall.

Color knowledge

Darker colors such as brown, black, or dark green give as good a view to the outside from the inside as do light colors; the ability to see in, however, is very limited with dark colors. On the other hand, these dark colors are always likely to fade to a certain extent from exposure to sunlight. Natural or white are always good and do not affect the view from either side.

This hanging curtain is both decorative and practical. It masks the view into the house but does not interfere with the view out. Many different threads and yarns are suitable for such a window decoration.

On the other hand, a vivid color can liven up a somewhat depressing house or apartment and, on a street where all the front doors are identical, act as a welcoming recognition point for family and friends. The windows in the front of your house are of critical importance in creating a harmonious whole with the rest of your house. Be careful, therefore, in choosing the color and look at it both from the inside and from the outside of your home.

Measure First

Before you begin to crochet a hanging curtain, the area in which it will hang must be measured. The curtain will be stretched between two metal rods. Look first to decide where these should be placed and, when you have decided this, do your measuring from those spots. Don't use plastic or wooden rods as they have a tendency to bend under tension.

The Illustrated Curtain

For this window decoration a double cotton thread was used, but something such as thin macramé cord would also be suitable. A number 4 (E) crochet hook is suitable.

Begin by making a chain the width of the window. Crochet, alternating 1 triple crochet and 1 chain so that 1 chain is skipped. The rod is pushed through this first round. If the rod is quite thick and your thread quite thin then crochet 2 or 3 chains between the triple crochets rather than 1. Continue in filet crochet, working according to the illustration on page 11. Turn each row with 4 chain stitches for the double crochet on the side with the chain. As in the illustration 1 section is filled in and there you must work double crochet in place of the chain. In this example 1 chain is crocheted between every double crochet which means crochet 1 double crochet at every filled hole so that 3 double crochets come next to each other in the filet pattern. If there are 2 or more chains worked between the double crochets then in the closed sections work the same number of double crochets as there are chains. In the example shown, the border is about 6 inches deep while the window itself is about 83 inches high. Crochet your border so that there is a good relationship between the border and the rest of the design. Crochet the border for the top of the window in the same way. Now the borders must be joined together which means the right length for the stripes must be determined first. There is a relatively simple way of figuring: subtract twice the height of the border from the total length of the window. Subtract 2 inches from the length that remains to allow for the stretching of the stripes. Attach your yarn at the first stitch of the last row of the first border. Crochet a chain with, if you want, picots placed along it, for example crochet 10 chain stitches, then 1 picot (3 chain, 1 slip stitch in the first chain), alternating 7 and 10 chains between the following picots.

Crochet to the right length and crochet a chain with a double crochet in the first double crochet of the last row of the second border. Crochet in the next chain of the border 1 double crochet and crochet 1 double crochet in the following double crochet. Now crochet the second chain and connect it to the first border with 1 double crochet; skip the chain stitch. Crochet 3 double crochets next to each other and continue to work in this manner on all chains so that the borders are joined along their entire widths. Finish off.

Filet Crochet

Filet crochet is sometimes also called netting. With this form of crochet square or rectangular holes can be formed. This is determined by the height of the crochet stitches and the width of the chains between these stitches. Every stitch larger than a single crochet – that is, for example, a half double crochet, a double crochet, a triple crochet, or a still larger stitch – can serve for the vertical bars while the vertical stitches are chains. Which are used depends on the height of the vertical sections and the desired shape of the holes.

Filet crochet is ideal for curtains in which designs taken from pictures are used. At one

time this type of design was used a good deal for crocheted bedspreads and for insertion in linens. There is some indication that the look is returning to fashion.
The technique is very simple and should pose no problems for a beginner.

Conventional Filet Work

Here we introduce filet crochet with square holes. Crochet a chain for the beginning, turn and crochet the first double crochet in the 8th chain from the end of the needle. This finishes the first hole, see picture 1. Crochet 2 chain stitches, skip 2 stitches of the chain and crochet in the following chain stitch a double crochet, see picture 2. Crochet in this way until the end of the chain and turn with 3 chain stitches in the first first double crochet. If the first hole is to be filled according to the illustration then crochet 2 double crochet in the 2 chains of the previous row, see picture 3. The following double crochet comes on the double crochet in the previous row, so there are 4 double crochets next to each other. Crochet for the following open hole 2 chains and 1 double crochet in the following double crochet and so forth. If after the following turn there is an open hole then, after the 3 chains of the turn, crochet 2 chains and then 1 double crochet on the following double crochet of the previous row; see picture 4.
With rectangular holes not 2 but 1 chain is crocheted between the double crochet or a triple crochet with 1 or 2 chains between every triple crochet. Triple crochet with 3 chains gives square holes.

Variations

If you follow the illustration but crochet closed areas where open areas are shown and close the open areas an entirely different effect is created. The border becomes more massive and the design is created by the openings in the border. Consider designing your own border. Use a piece of graph paper for this. Graph paper can be found in stationery and school supply stores. Figure out the number of rows that are needed for

Filet crochet is made this way.

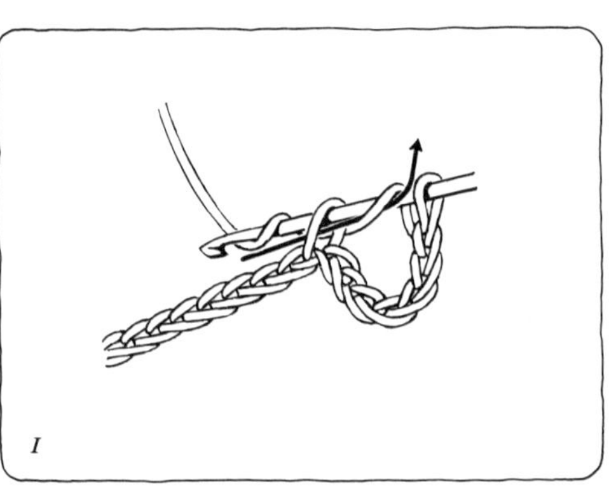

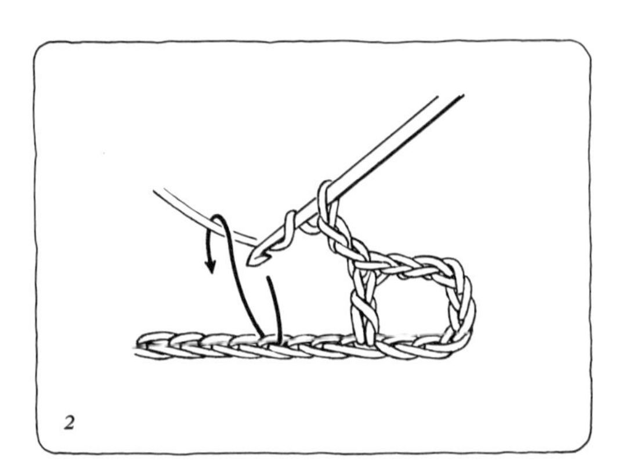

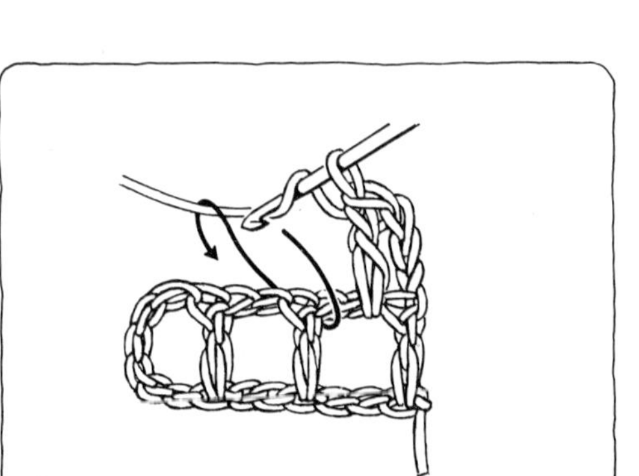

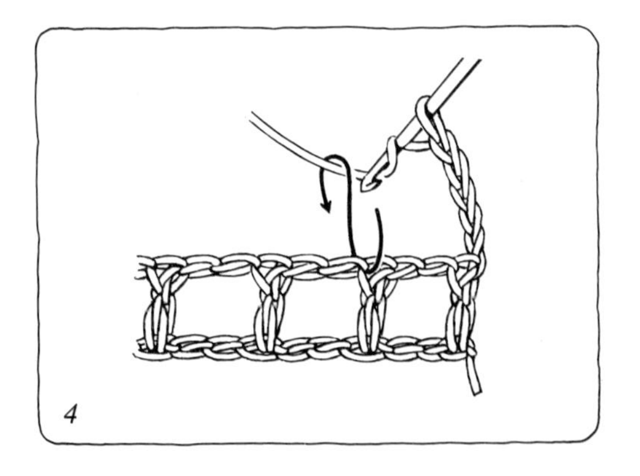

the height of the border. Make the first and last rows without a design, that is, either entirely of open holes or entirely worked in double crochet. Design a border on which the individual motifs are such that they can be repeated over and over. You can get good ideas for this from the simple borders used for cross stitch. Such a curtain can be used not only as a window decoration but also, for example, to make a screen for a room or on the inside of the glass doors of older kitchen cabinets. If you have a viewless window that faces a blank wall, consider using this for cheerful window curtains.

If you would prefer to have the openings between the stripes with picot edging somewhat larger, it is easy to do. Rather than working 3 double crochet between the chains work 6 double crochet and use a single thread of cotton or thinner yarn.

For a *glass door*, such as a swinging door in the hall, the picots can be replaced with beads. Tack the beads to the ball of yarn and crochet the beads, randomly spaced, at the same time as the chain is crocheted. Choose beads the same color as the yarn or slightly darker or lighter.

With a *room screen* you can add a third border right in the middle between the top and the bottom border. Crochet a chain attaching the bottom border to this middle border to the top border.

This can also be used for a hanging curtain next to the front door. If the curtain is crocheted from a fine yarn you can even use, in place of a simple design, the name of the people who live there. You can be able to find simple letters that are suitable for this in cross stitch books.

Curtains of this kind for the kitchen windows or the kitchen door will give your home an entirely new look. It is best to give these some color, especially if the kitchen itself is dark.

The vertical lines of every square indicate the double crochets while the horizontal lines show the chains between the double crochets. The filled in spaces show double crochets which are worked on the chains.

For a small window

As well as picture windows and other single pane windows there are other windows

Make a separate little curtain for every pane of glass. From outside the panes look as if they are made of cut glass. The instructions for these are on this page.

You can make a splendid window decoration by working the star design of the small window curtains. The design is as effective here on its own as in the panes of the larger window opposite.

which are divided by strips of wood into smaller panes. Here, too, the usual curtains can as often as not be replaced by an attractive window decoration. The crochet work for such a decoration should be worked so that it forms a sort of spider web. The picture on page 12 is a good example of this. The work is stretched by means of screws which are put into crocheted loops so every pane can be decorated.

For such a decoration any pattern for a small round crocheted work can be used. On the last round loops of chain stitches are crocheted the right length for stretching.

The illustrated pattern is made for a window measuring about 13¼ by 16¼ inches in each pane. Use a fine crochet thread that is suitable to use with a number 2 (C) crochet hook. If you want the design to be somewhat larger, then use a thicker yarn and a number 6 crochet hook. The design is worked from the middle out.

Crochet a chain of 10 stitches and close it into a ring with a slip stitch.

Round 1. Crochet 20 double crochet in the ring, crochet as the 1st double crochet 3 chains and close the round with a slip stitch in the 3rd chain from the beginning.

Round 2. Crochet 2 double crochets in every double crochet of the previous round, then after each 2nd double crochet two chains. Use both loops of the double crochet of the previous round. There are now 10 groups of 2 double crochet with 2 chains in between. This is the beginning of the star pattern which has 10 points.

Round 3. Crochet 1 double crochet in every double crochet and crochet over the 2 chain stitches 4 chain stitches again creating 10 groups of 2 double crochet with 4 chains between each group.

In the next round every star point must grow wider. Do this by crocheting an additional double crochet after each of the double crochet groups. The beginning of each row is in the middle of a group of double crochet.

Round 4. Crochet 10 times 4 double crochet with 4 chains.

Round 5. Crochet 10 times 6 double crochet with 4 chains.

Round 6. Crochet 10 times 7 double crochet with 4 chains. This is the middle of each point, which is why only 1 more double crocheted is worked. In the following rounds each point must grow smaller but, to keep the work flat, more chains must be crocheted between the points.

Round 7. 10 times 6 double crochet and 6 chains. The double crochets must be worked exactly over the middle of each group.

Round 8. 10 times 5 double crochets and 8 chains.

Round 9. 10 times 4 double crochets and 10 chains.

Round 10. 10 times 3 double crochets and 19 chains.

These 19 chains are for the points above the star motif.

Round 11. Crochet 1 double crochet in every chain of the arch and in the middle chain of every arch of 19 chain stitches crochet for the point 3 double crochets. Crochet 1 double crochet on the 3 double crochets of the star points. The star motif is

These pictures show another possibility for the star design. Work the smaller version in a finer thread or yarn than the medium and larger ones. You can also bring your imagination to bear on the colors. More in this chapter.

now finished. Around this motif a border must be crocheted so the design can be stretched. Begin in the middle of the 3 double crochets that are worked in the middle of the large arch. Crochet 1 single crochet on this middle double crochet then 20 chain stitches and 1 single crochet on the middle double crochet of the following arch crocheting in this way throughout the round and closing the circle with a slip stitch in the 1st single crochet.

Following row: crochet alternating 1 double crochet and 2 chains thereby omitting 2 chains. On every arch there will be 7 double crochet. Crochet above the point – this is a single crochet – 3 chains and crochet further on the following arch working about 7 double crochet.

Last row: this is where the stretch section will be crocheted. You can best decide for yourself what the length should be. Begin with a chain which you end, when it has reached double length, on the 3 stitches of the point with a double crochet. Work to the following point, crochet double crochet on double crochet with 2 chain stitches in between. Finish with a double crochet in the 3 chains of the following point. Again crochet a chain the right length and fasten it securely with a double crochet in the same 3 chains.

Crochet the entire round in this way with a chain of stitches at every point. These can vary in size depending on the size of the window.

Other Uses for the Star Design

The pattern, crocheted with thick cotton, can be used as a doily. For this, work the first 12 rounds as described and then crochet a round of, for example, picot stitch as a finish.

The pattern can be used as a cover for a *round cushion.* For this you can use more color. For example, you can work the first 10 rounds of the star in one color, the point border in another color, and the finishing round in a third color. You might like to work in shades of one color from dark to light or the reverse. Choose a color that complements the color of the crochet for the cushion itself.

Window stretchers. You may be able to find round window stretchers or improvise them from, perhaps, embroidery hoops. You can have a splendid looking window by using three different sizes one above the other. For the smallest, crochet a star design from fine yarn, for the middle size crochet a somewhat larger design from thicker thread, and for the largest make a still larger design from still thicker thread. You can change not only the thickness of your thread or yarn but also the color and add to the drama of the decoration. These were but a few suggestions. There are naturally hundreds more.

You can make yourself a window stretcher by making a picture frame and stretching your design in it. This stretching can be done by boring small holes in the frame and running through these and through the work a crocheted chain. If you aren't handy, you can buy a frame ready-made or look for an old one of the right size.

Make your own window stretcher! Make a wooden frame and bore holes into it at regular distances so the crochet work can be stretched in it with a crocheted cord. The picture illustrates 2 ways in which a frame can be held to dry after gluing.

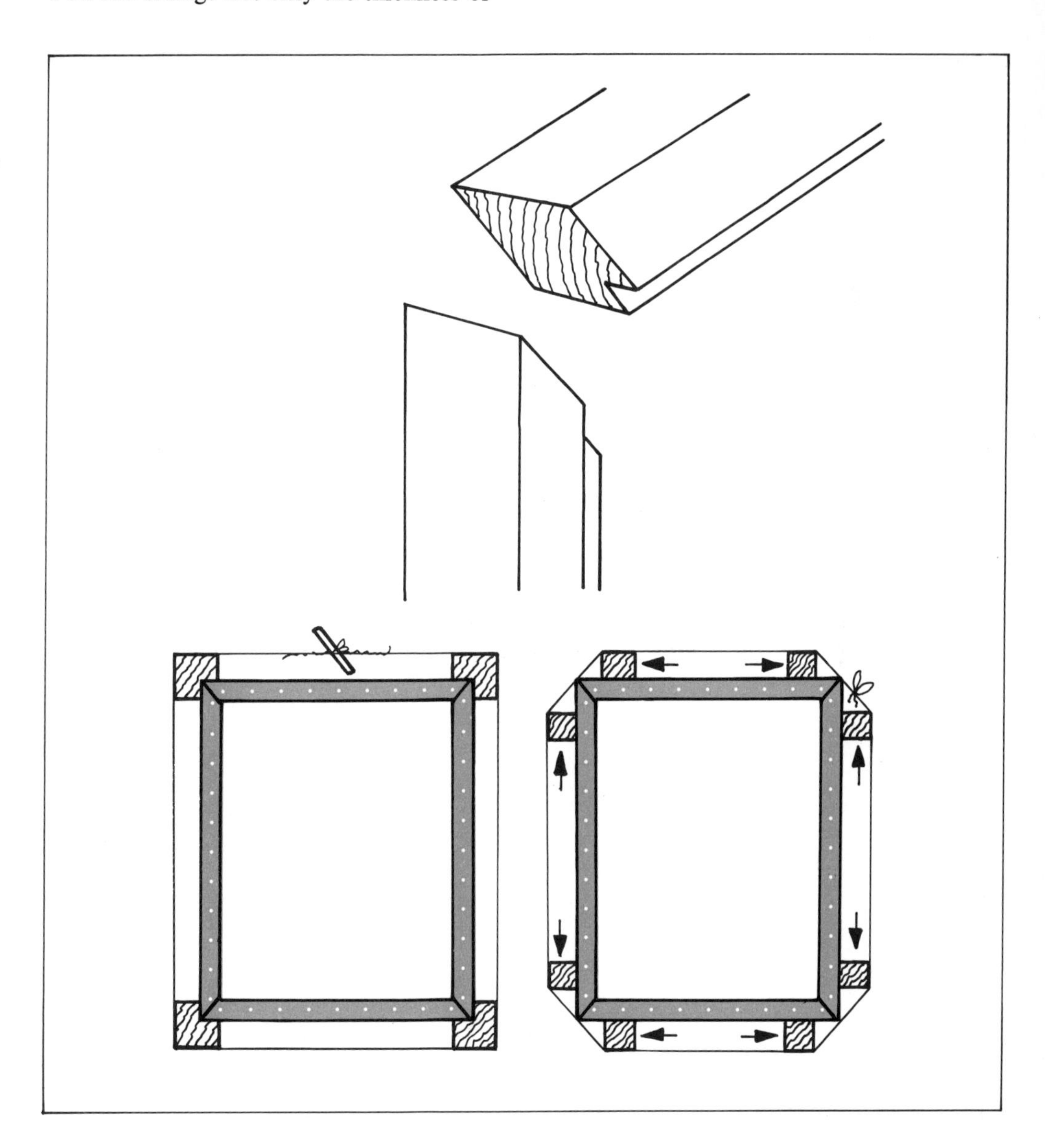

2 For Window and Table

In addition to window decorations such as were shown in the last chapter, you can also make under curtains and valances with crochet. These are also a sort of window decoration which take the place of the traditional glass curtains. These often result in a more home-like atmosphere when they are crocheted because the resulting fabric is always rougher than in the case of glass curtains. In the past, crocheted curtains were almost always made of white cotton but today there is a wider choice of color, color is very much part of our lives, and you should probably use color in your curtains. There is also more choice in the yarns and threads for crocheting. The curtains which are shown, for example, are crocheted with a thread made of a combination of linen and cotton. This thread is used mainly for weaving but the result with crochet – using a large crochet hook – will prove most successful.

The colors of the threads are attractive and the combination of colors is excellent.

Here's a different looking under curtain! A fine yarn, designed for weaving, was used to make it. The hook was a coarse one. The top part is worked in filet crochet. The border with the rosettes can be used in many other ways.

Other Yarns and Threads
If the curtains are crocheted with a heavy cotton yarn and a larger crochet hook the design will be larger and have a heavier structure; see the picture at the right for an example of this. This works well at a window where you don't want anyone to be able to see in.
Synthetic yarns can also be used although you may have trouble finding these specific color combinations in these yarns.

Other Colors
Naturally you can use other colors. The curtain has a basic color which is used for the top half of the curtain, which is worked in filet work, and which is picked up again in the border. Use a light color for this, such as ecru, very light yellow, or light beige. In the border itself two shades of green, rose red, and yellow are combined. Choose four colors that fit the interior of your room. Pick a dark color such as brown to go with the wood of the furnitures and a bright color for the rosettes; the other two colors must, naturally, harmonize with these two colors. The amount of yarn that you'll need depends on the size of the window and the type of yarn you are using.

Measure first
The width of the curtain – the part above the border – is the same as the width of the window. Measure, then make a test sample in filet crochet about 4 inches wide. Begin with a chain of stitches, crocheted fairly loosely. Start the first round in the 7th chain stitch from the needle and crochet 1 double crochet, 1 chain, skip 1 stitch of the chain, crochet in the next stitch 1 double crochet, 1 chain, skip 1 chain and so forth until the end of the chain. Crochet 1 double crochet in the last stitch. Turn with 4 chain stitches and crochet 1 double crochet in every double crochet of the previous row with 1 chain between each double crochet. After 6 rows place the work flat on a table and count the number of stitches in 4 inches. If, for instance, there are 40 stitches, counting both double crochets and chains, then there are 10 stitches to 1 inch. If the curtain has to be 36 inches wide, the figuring is simple: 36 times 10 is 360 stitches. This gives you the number of stitches on the starting chain; remember to crochet 4 additional chains for turning. See the instructions for filet crochet on page 10.
The crocheting of a test sample is extremely important because the curtains must hang smoothly at the bottom.
The pictured border is about 12 inches deep, subtract this and the height of the filet crochet from the total length of the curtain

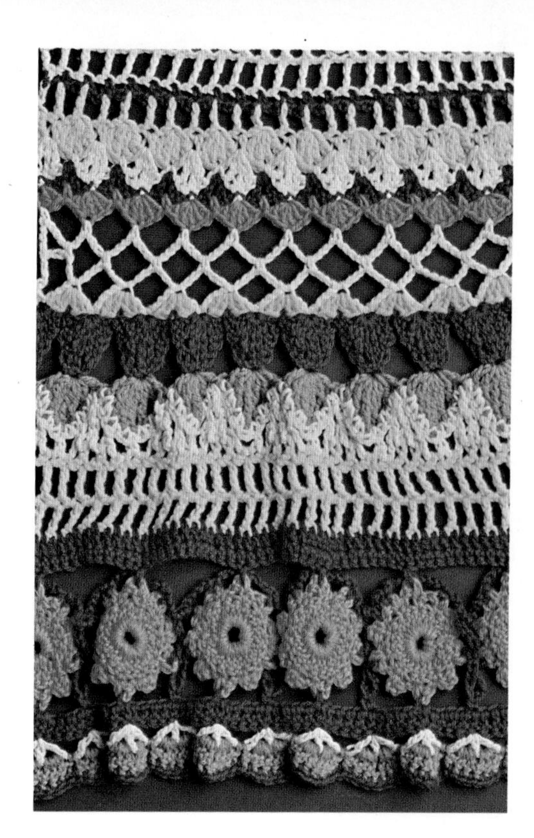

Here is the same curtain as seen on the left hand page worked in other colors and materials. This time it is crocheted in cotton and is suitable for a border on a table cloth (see also page 20).

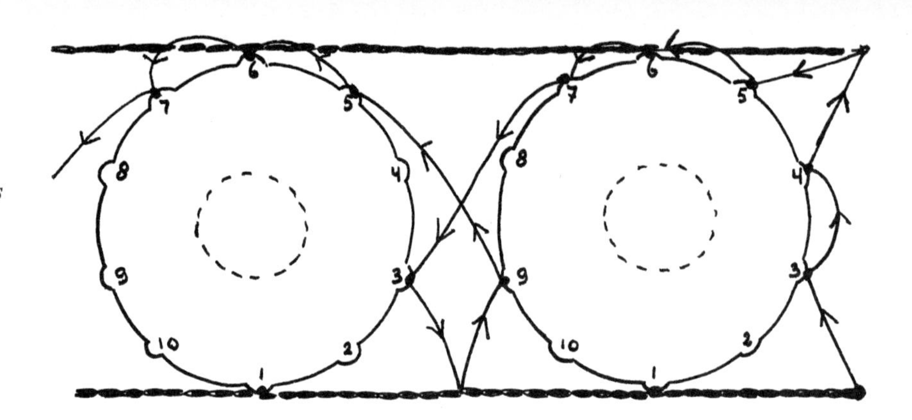

This drawing shows how the rosette border on the curtain must be worked. Begin at the bottom right and follow the direction of the arrows. The lines indicate chains, the points are single crochets.

to get the measurement for the top of the curtain. The top of the curtain has been hung with large rings placed on a rod but there are many other possible ways of hanging curtains. If the window is not too wide a thin round wooden rod can be used.

The Border

The complete instructions for making this will be found on page 95.
If you want to make only the border to use as a valance, first work about 3 rows of filet crochet; this is needed to hang the valance and to establish the right width.
The border can be worked in two colors: a basic color for the border with the rosettes in a contrasting color. The border itself is actually in two parts, so you can use only one part of it, for instance as a border on a round cloth for a garden table. For this, you would work the first 12 rows of the border. The difference between working this border and the border for the curtain is that for this one you would work in the round to avoid a seam.

Triple crochet.
Wrap the thread around the hook twice before putting it into the stitch.

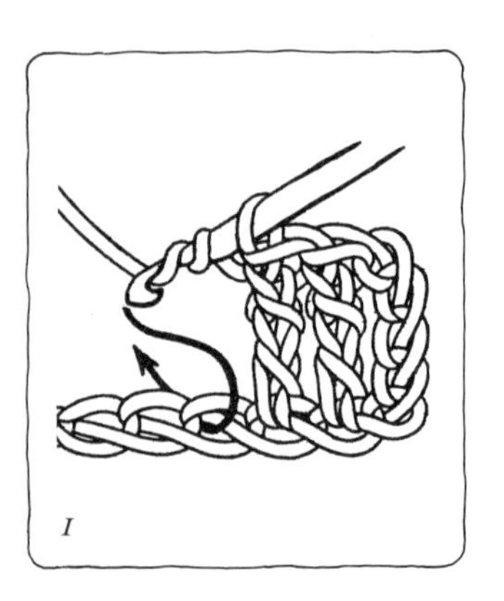

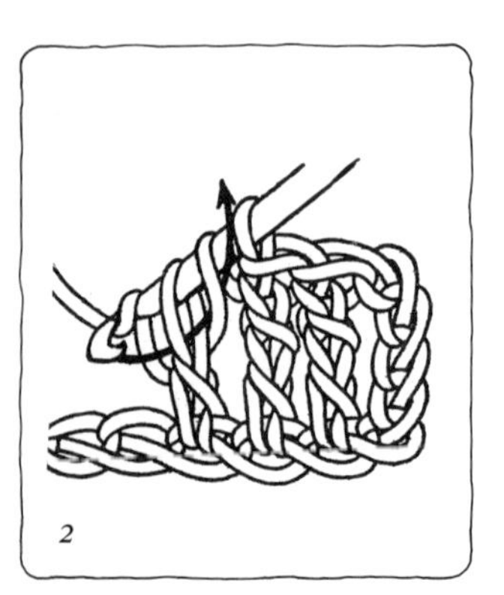

Border for a cloth (see photo on page 20).
Measure the circumference of the table and crochet a chain the same length. Be sure that the number of stitches is an even number. Close the chain into a ring with a slip stitch. Crochet 3 chains as the 1st double crochet and after that work 1 double crochet in every chain stitch. Close the round with a slip stitch in the 3rd stitch from the first double crochet. Now work the border. Crochet 3 chains at the beginning of the round for the first double crochet and, when you are working single crochet, 1 chain stitch. Close every round with a slip stitch. Finish after 12 rounds.

Changing Colors

In order to get a proper transition from one color to the next you should finish the last stitch of the first color with the following color. This sounds complicated but is simple. You must do the last pulling through of the yarn in a double crochet while there are still 2 loops on the hook. Then take the next color, wrap this around the needle, and pull through both loops.
To change with single crochet, put the hook in the last stitch and pick up a stitch then, with the new color, work the single crochet, see illustrations 1, 2, and 3.
In illustration 4 you can see how the thread must be finished off. Use a needle to weave this into the horizontal stitches, fitting the color to the yarn or thread. Do this while you are crocheting, after every row.

Variations

Do you consider the bottom part of the border, the rosette border, more attractive than the other section as an edge for a tablecloth? Then use that. Begin as in the first border: measure the circumference, crochet a chain, and crochet on this 1 row of double crochet in the round. Crochet in the following row in every double crochet 1 single crochet, close the round, and finish off. Now crochet the rosettes separately; see the description of how to work the doily. The 20th round in the text becomes in this case the 2nd round, thus the single crochet round. In order to have the right number of rosettes it is adviseable to sew the crocheted border of 2 rounds to the cloth so that the circle can lie flat. Place the rosettes around the cloth, leaving between each one about 5 inches open. This particular crochet work is not really suitable for beginners although they are welcome to try it and may succeed with it.

Finishing

How is the border sewn to the cloth? Cut out a piece of linen the circumference of the table top plus $\frac{3}{4}$ inch for a seam. Baste, then sew, a $\frac{1}{2}$ inch hem with a $\frac{1}{4}$ inch turn-under. Sew the crocheted border on top of the hem.

Crocheting and applying at the same time

This can also be done. Make the cloth as above, leaving a seam allowance of about $\frac{1}{2}$ inch. Crochet a round of single crochet over this allowance, using a metal crochet hook with a sharp point. When that is done, crochet the 1st round of the border, the double crochet round.

A round pillow

Round pillows for chairs (see page 20) can be crocheted with the border.
For the middle of the pillow cover crochet a rosette; make this 1 round of double crochet larger than it is with the border. Increase with double crochet in this round so the rosette lies flat. Crochet around the rosette a row of chain stitches and single crochets; work the single crochet at the points. Next, crochet a round of single crochet and bind off. Crochet the small rosettes as for the border and arrange a number of them around the middle rosette, placing them only slightly apart. Work chain stitches and single crochet around the outside of the row in order to connect and finish the outside edge. Now, crochet the chains between the rosettes, joining these to the inside border; in this case, of course, to the outside round of the middle rosette.
Be sure the cover stays flat by crocheting more stitches on the outside edge of the rosette border than on the border of the curtain. Cover a round, plump cushion with fabric in a coordinating color and sew the crochet cover to that.

Under curtains for a wide window

If a window is very wide and high under curtains crocheted in panels can be very decorative. Panels will make the area seem less large and you will give your windows an original effect. This design comes from Sweden, where crocheted window curtains are very popular. At first glance it appears to be a crochet technique very much like filet work, but it is a variation which also creates holes which are wider and less high. The curves between double crochets are chains and single crochets. This variation gives the crochet a softer look than classic filet work (see photo on page 21).
Every panel is about 10 inches wide and 17 inches high. You can modify the height easily by making more rows above the crocheted flower design.
How to crochet these curtains will be found at the back of the book.
Choose a smooth cotton yarn and a medium

These four illustrations show how colors can be changed at the end of a row. For more information on this, see the page to the left.

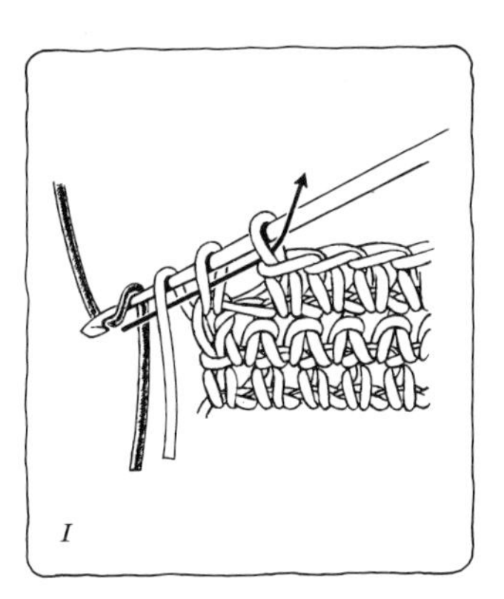

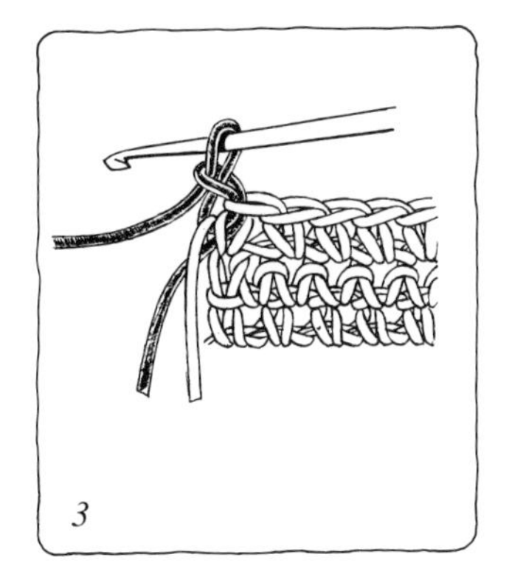

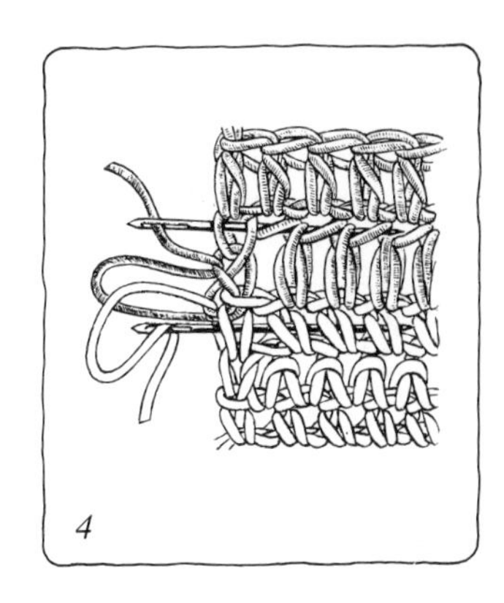

size crochet hook. If you crochet very loosely, then, of course, you will use a finer crochet hook.
Around each panel a border is crocheted from double crochets and picots, after which the sections are crocheted together.
If you have a narrow window, but like this design, try to work out an adaptation of it. Measure the width of the window and divide it into 2 or 3 panels. Keep the measurements in proportion and plan to use on top a not-too-heavy rod. If the window is divided, then make one panel for each separate pane.

Hanging the curtain
Each panel has 2 large rings sewn to it that will pass over a thick rod. There are many kinds of drapery and curtain rods available in the stores today, one of which should be right for the look you want. With a wide window you must be sure to use a very sturdy rod to avoid having it sag in the middle. If the window is not so wide, then a thinner rod can be chosen and each panel should probably hang from more than 2 rings.

A large window
If you like the look of these curtains but feel that panels are not right for your window, crochet one large curtain.
In order to get the flower placed properly on the curtain you must first measure. Measure the width of the window and crochet a sample piece in the basic stitch; this you can find in the instructions and you need only read and crochet the first 4 rows. In the curtain in the picture, every panel is 73 stitches wide. The double crochet on either

This garden table cloth has been decorated with the crocheted border from the under curtains on page 16. The pillow cover is made from the rosette border of the same curtains. For how to information, see the instruction pages.

These curtains, worked in panels, come from Sweden. The number of panels depends on the width of the window. For instructions, see page 19.

side of each panel must, when you are making one large curtain, naturally be omitted and only used at each end of the curtain. In other words there are 65 stitches needed per panel and per flower motif. Make a chain the number of stitches you need, divisible by 65, plus 8 stitches for the double crochet on each side. Keep your stitch sample in mind and make any corrections necessary. At the end of the chain crochet 2 extra chains to turn. The first double crochet after the turn is worked in the 4th chain from the crochet hook. The flower motif is found in the instructions at row 34.

Finishing. Crochet a border of double crochet and picots as described for the panels along the bottom of this large curtain.

The chart. There is also a chart given here of the flower design. More variations can be crocheted using this picture. Crochet a square with the motif or make it entirely in filet work. You should find it easy to work out your own changes in this.

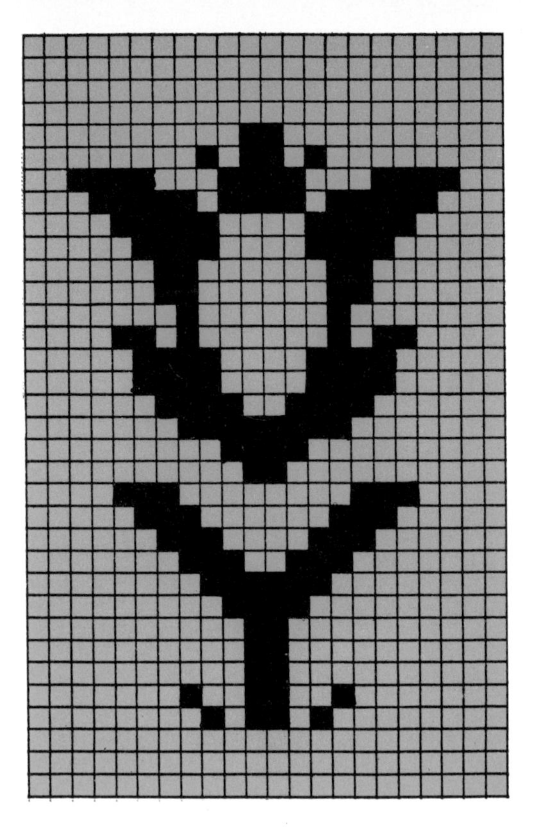

There are many possibilities in this pattern. You can see one on page 24, worked in filet crochet and stretched in a wood frame, but the design can also be used to crochet a spread made up of these blocks which are sewn together.

What can be made with the square?

A lovely window or wall decoration, such as a dark crocheted object in a wooden frame against a light wall, or a light crocheted object in a light frame against a dark wall. The squares can also be sewn together and used for a spread. Either technique – the variation on filet crochet or the classic technique – can be used for these. The motif, crocheted with very fine crochet yarn, can be worked in a series of squares, for example 3 wide and 3 high to decorate a cushion. Don't use white for this. There are so many other beautiful colors that are especially suitable for cushions. A dark corner of the room can be perked up with the right cushion.

Be adventurous with this design and crochet some samples with different kinds of yarns and with different colors. You'll be pleased with the results.

Increasing and decreasing in filet crochet

1. increasing 1 hole (square) at the beginning of the round. Crochet 7 chains and crochet a double crochet on the first double crochet of the previous row.
2. increasing 1 hole (square) at the end of the row. Crochet 2 chains, wrap your thread around the hook 2 times as for a triple crochet, and put the hook in the bottom of the last worked double crochet.
3. Wrap yarn around hook and bind off 1 stitch.
4. Wrap yarn around the hook and bind off 2 stitches.
5. Wrap yarn around the hook and bind off 2 more stitches.
6. Wrap yarn around the hook and bind off the last 2 stitches.

Increasing in a solid block

7. Crochet 5 chains at the beginning of the row where you will increase the solid block, then crochet 1 double crochet in the 4th and 1 double crochet in the 5th chain from the crochet hook and 1 double crochet in the following double crochet. At the end of the round wrap the yarn around the hook twice and put the hook into the bottom of the last double crochet.
8. Wrap the yarn around the hook and pull it through 2 loops.
9. Again wrap the yarn around the hook and pull it through 2 loops.
10. Wrap the yarn around the hook and put it through the last loops.
11. Repeat instructions 7 through 10 two more times.

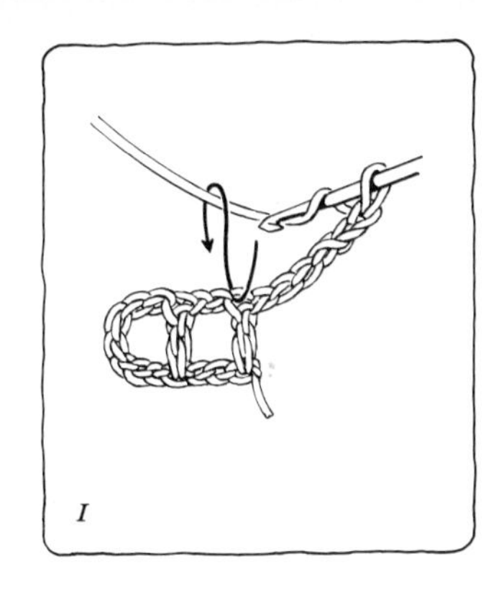

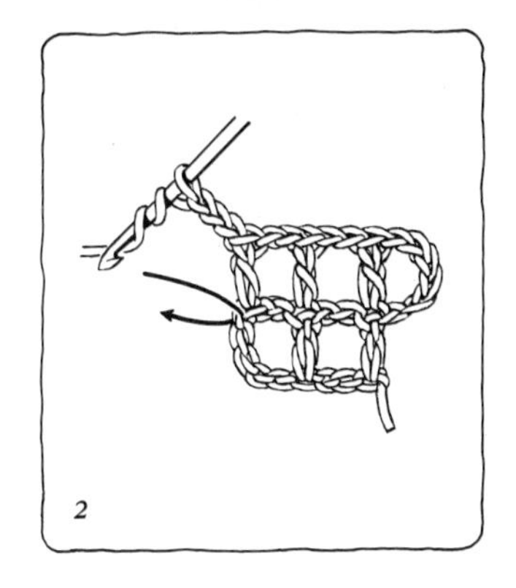

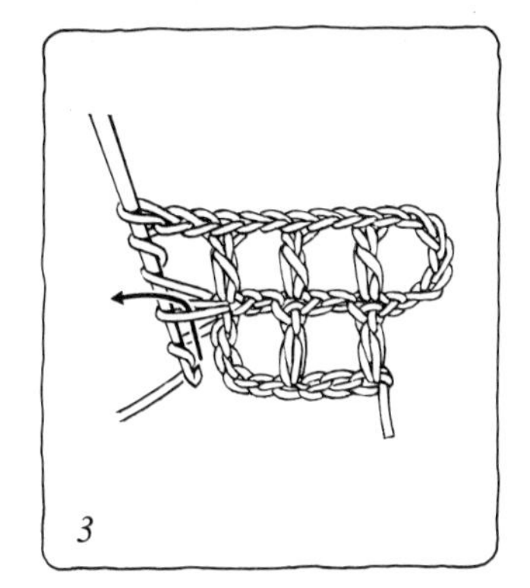

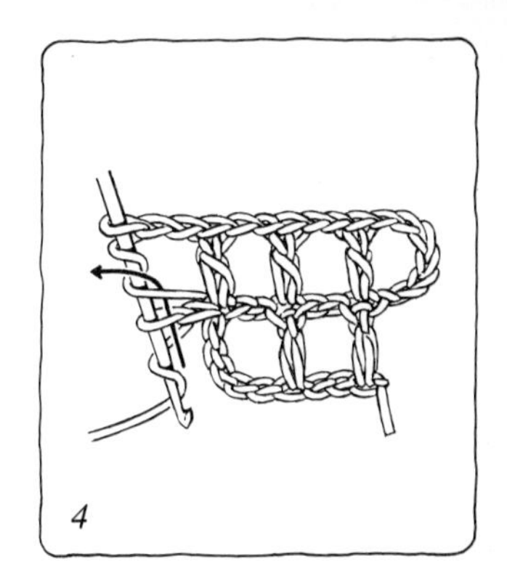

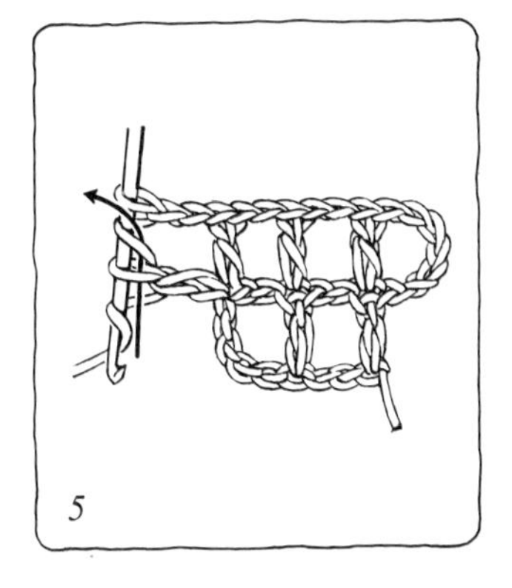

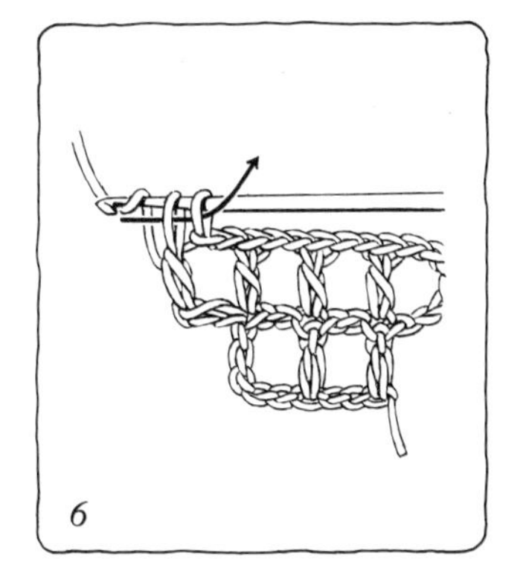

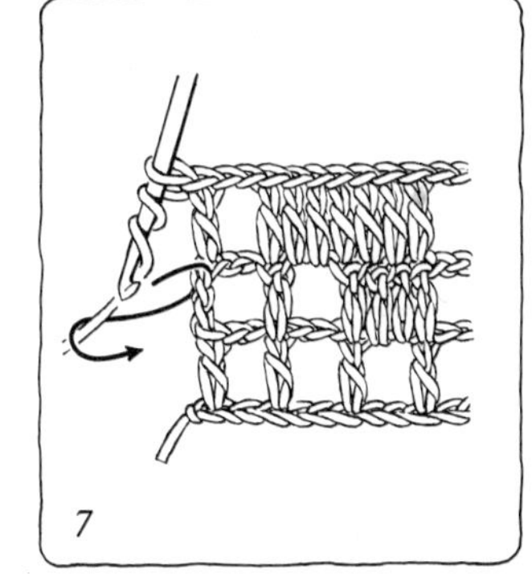

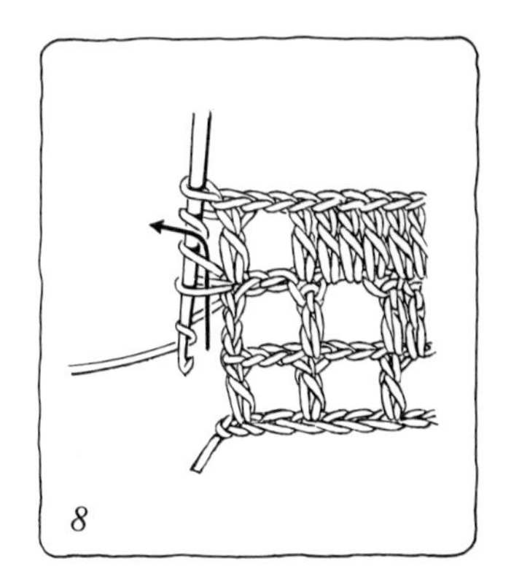

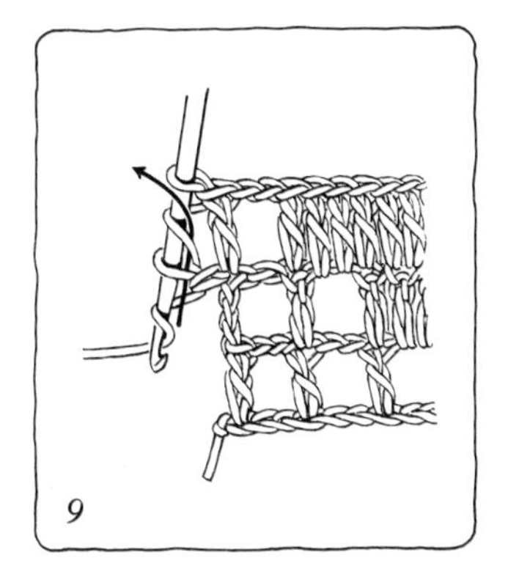

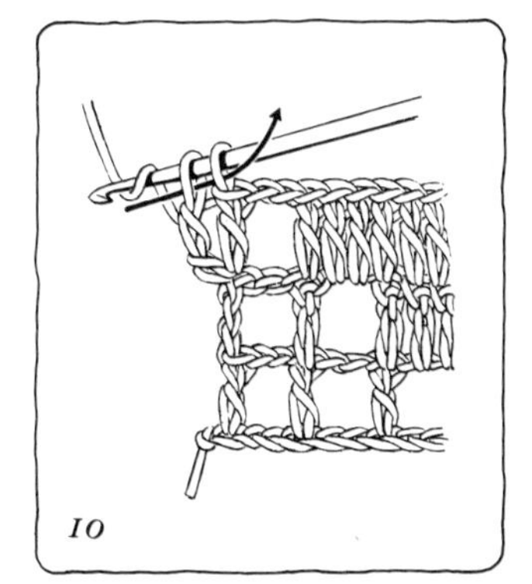

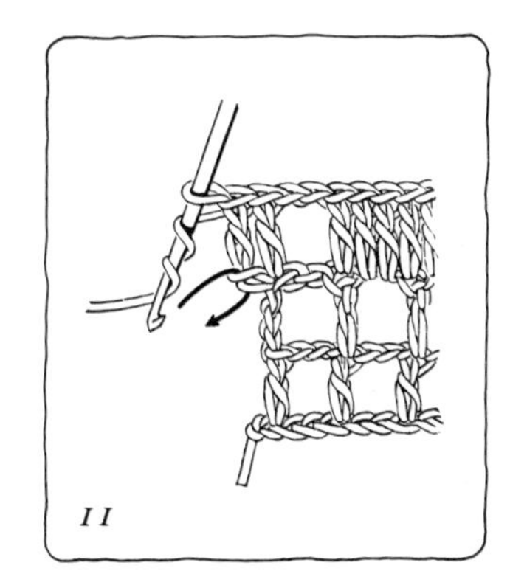

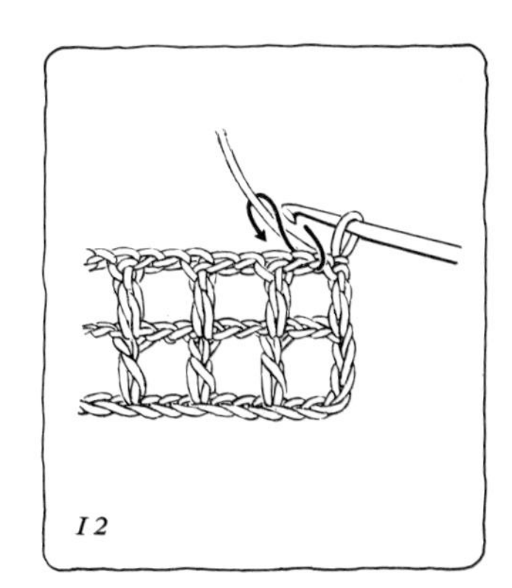

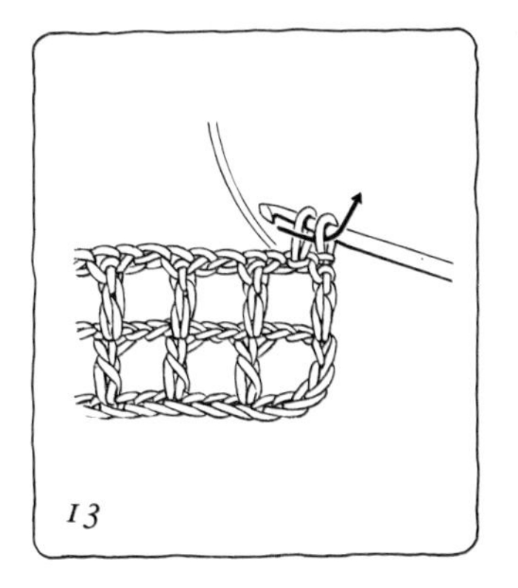

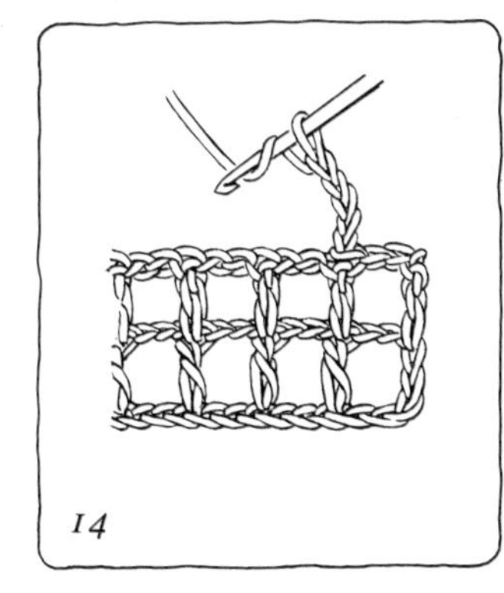

Increasing and decreasing in filet crochet.

Illustrations 1 through 6 show increasing with open blocks.

Illustrations 7 through 11 show increasing with closed blocks.

Illustrations 12 through 14 show decreasing.

Decreasing on both sides

12. If 1 hole (square) must be decreased. Crochet 1 chain. Make a slip stitch in the 1st chain.
13. Crochet a slip stitch in the 2nd chain.
14. Crochet a slip stitch on the double crochet, crochet for the next hole 5 chains, and crochet a double crochet on the following double crochet. At that end of the row decrease by turning for the last square on the double crochet next to last. If more squares must be decreased at the beginning or end of the row, then make a slip stitch to the point, crochet further, and turn at the end of the row.

Combining fabric and crochet

This valance is really not suitable for the windows of a house but makes a nice decoration on the top of a door opening which has café doors. Crochet the flower motifs first and then cut the scallops from the fabric. The size of each flower determines the width and depth of the scallops.

The flower design shown in the pattern on page 22 and made into a window or wall decoration.

The bottom of a *roller blind* can be beautifully decorated with these scallops and crocheted flowers. This gives a very different effect from the usual roller blind, especially when the blind is raised. If you want to hide the drapery rod behind a wood or fabric cover decorated with the drapery fabric you can finish this cover with the crocheted flowers and scallops. Make sure the scallops can be seen from the outside.

Yarn or thread

Choose crochet yarn that goes with your fabric. Heavy fabric needs heavier yarn than lighter fabric. A woolen fabric works best with woolen yarn or with an attractive heavy silk yarn.

Colors

The colors must suit the colors of the fabric. Pick up one color from the fabric and have the other colors harmonize with this. The curtain in the picture is orange with light yellow and yellow. You could use dark green and light green with a medium green, or dark green with orange, or brownish yellow with gold and moss green. You must always use a contrasting color for the second group of petals if the design is to look right. This color is repeated in the tassels.

Crocheting the flower

Begin with the color for the center, in this case light yellow. Crochet a chain of 8 stitches and close it into a ring with a slip stitch. Crochet 12 single crochets in the chain. Always crochet 1 chain as the first single crochet. End the row with a slip stitch in the first chain. In the following row crochet 16 single crochet by working 2 single crochet in every 3rd single crochet. Work this through both loops of the stitch below. Close every round with a slip stitch in the first chain. Last round for the center: chain 5, * 1 double crochet, 2 chain, repeat from* in every following single crochet of the previous round. Close the round with a slip stitch in the 2nd chain from the beginning. There are now 16 double crochets between 16 arches of 3 chains. End.

A fabric valance with scallops decorated with tassels and colored crocheted flowers in each scallop.

Finishing the scallop border with blanket stitch.

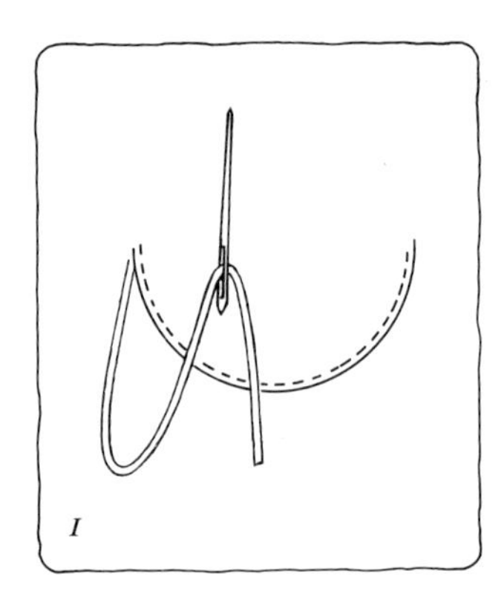

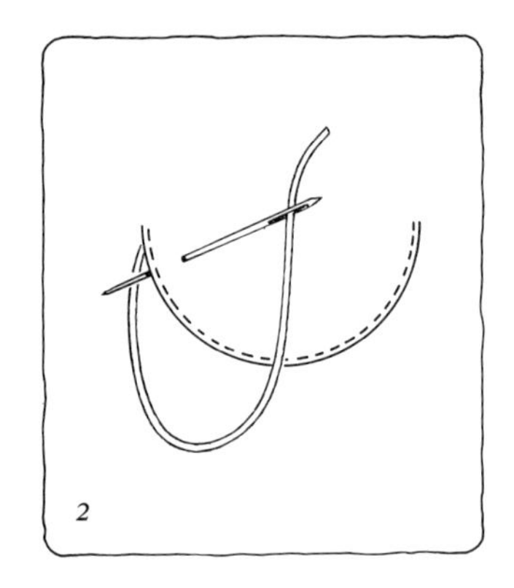

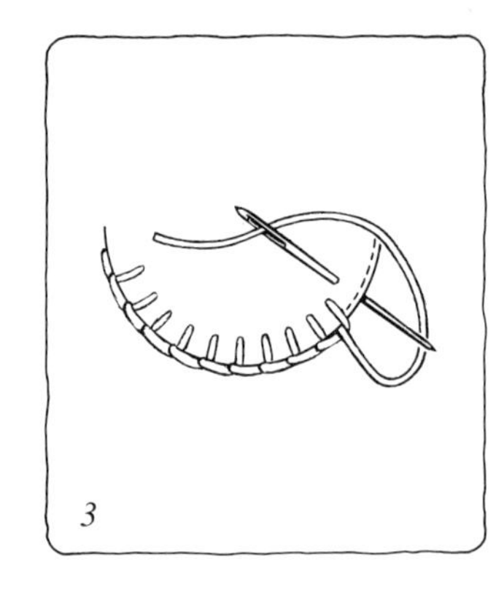

Illustrations A, B, and C; making tassels as a finishing touch.

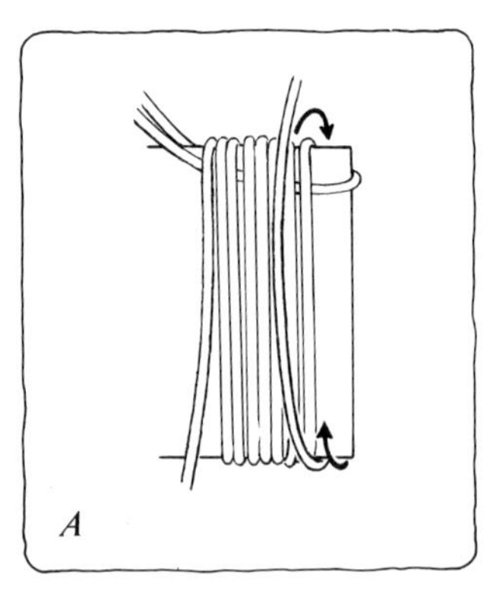

Begin with orange. Crochet 2 chains,* 12 chains, turn, crochet on the chain: 1 slip stitch, 1 single crochet, and 10 double crochet, skip the following 2 chains, 1 single crochet in the following 2 chains, repeat from*. Close the round with a slip stitch. There are now 8 half petals.
Crochet along the other side of the chain of 10 stitches 10 double crochet, 1 single crochet, and slip stitch. You are now at the top of the petal. Crochet along the other side of the petal making a slip stitch in every stitch on the underside, repeat from and close the round with a slip stitch. End.

The scallops
Measure the diameter of the flower. Make a circle the same size from heavy paper and use this as a pattern to draw the scallops on the fabric. Be sure they are the same distance apart. Baste a basting thread through the fabric with the grain to indicate the height of the scallops, indicating how they are separated. Indicate the center of every arch. Draw a line at the center of the paper circle and put the points together. Draw around the entire circle with tailors' chalk. Baste another thread along the bottom of the circle and baste another thread in the middle of the two threads and parallel to them.
Put the paper circle against the bottom basting thread; the top of the circle will be against the top basting thread. Draw around the circle with chalk. The circles should connect; if they don't because of the width of your fabric, place them further apart. Baste the scallops so that the top of the half circle is joined to the bottom of the next circle. Remove the remaining basting threads. Next, with the sewing machine, run small stitches in thread the same color as the fabric along the wavy line to prevent raveling.
Next, using the same thread you are using for the crochet in the color of the fabric work blanket stitches over the basting thread and machine stitches. See pictures 1, 2, and 3. If the fabric is not one that ravels and the crochet hook can go through it easily you can work a border of single crochet instead

Illustrations D, E, and F; inserting threads or yarns to make fringe.

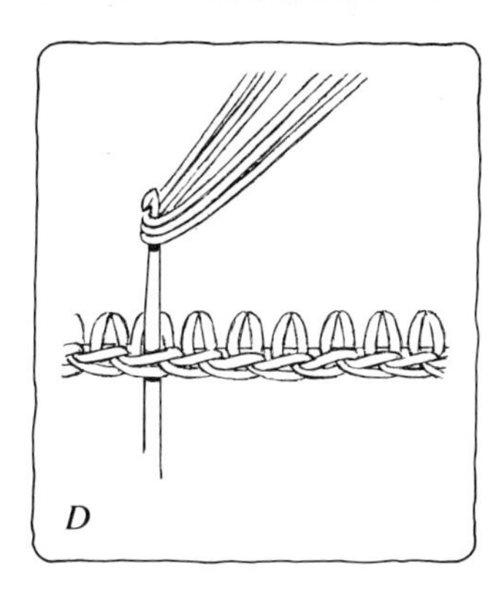

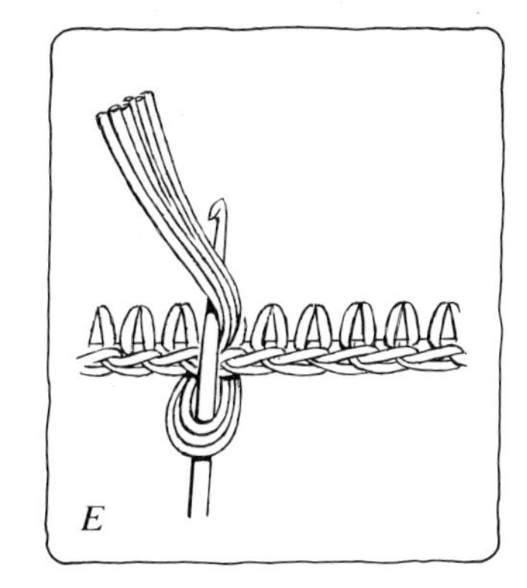

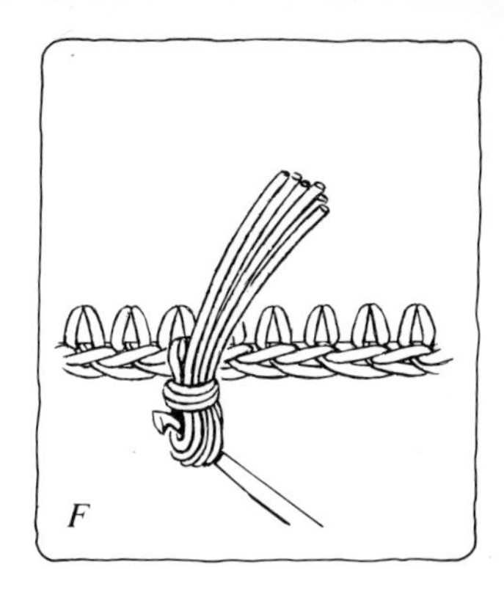

Illustrations G and H; knotting the strands of the fringe together.

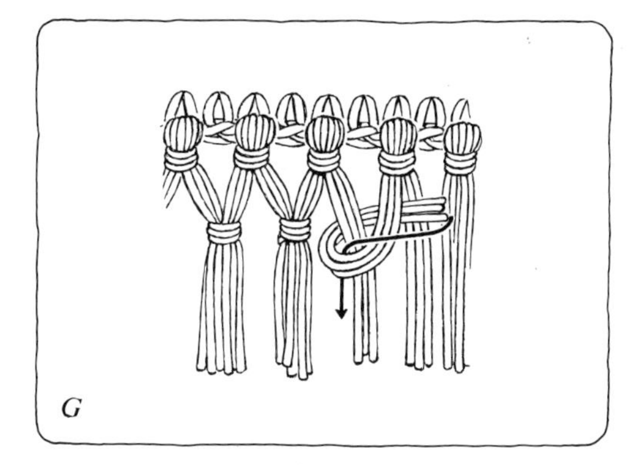

of the blanket stitch. Cut the remaining fabric away carefully with a sharp pair of scissors; if you plan to crochet the edge, cut the fabric away first.

Making fringe

Cut a strip of cardboard as wide as the desired length of the fringe and about 6 inches long. Wrap a thread over the length of the cardboard and then wrap around the width with crochet yarn (see illustration A), until the right thickness for your tassel is reached. Pull the lengthwise thread to the top and knot it securely around the yarn. Pull out the cardboard and cut through the loops at the bottom; see illustration B. Wrap the tassel with crochet yarn at the top and tie securely; see picture C.

This brings us to other types of fringe decoration for crochet. The tassel can also be knotted. Cut threads from the crochet yarn that are twice as long as the desired length of the tassel. Take a group of 4 to 6 strands. Work these with a crochet hook through the stitches of, for example, a crocheted window valance. See illustrations D, E, and F. Knot the groups of yarn to each other; see illustrations G and H for how to do this. Finally, take half of each tassel and knot it to half of the tassel next to it.

3 The Dining Area

Come sit down on this long crocheted cushion and relax. The table is set for one, but there is always room for two.
The cushion is crocheted in filet crochet, chains of stitches braided through the length and the width, a pattern which forms an attractive texture for the cushion.

Colors
We chose orange for this dining corner with various hues of yellow and green as accent colors. To play with color it's important to know the rules of the game. The creation of a warm atmosphere in the eating area of a house – or anywhere else in your home – is not merely a matter of burning candles and providing a good cup of coffee. An interior can be arranged so it should be attractive, the colors can be well chosen, but if there is some wrong note, such as small objects which clash with the color scheme, it will still not be a success. Brown and beige are colors which go well together, but if they are used *alone* they will prove dull because they really demand another color.

What we know about color
How do you work out a color scheme to create the mood you want?

Primary colors
These are red, yellow, and blue. Put these 3 colors in a circle.

Secondary colors
Put green between yellow and blue in the circle, because it is made from a mixture of blue and yellow.
Violet comes between blue and red, because it is made up of these colors.
Orange goes between red and yellow, because it is made up of a mixture of these two colors.
Now move around the circle, beginning with yellow. Moving in a counter-clockwise direction next to yellow comes orange and then red. Violet is directly across from yellow, blue directly across from orange, and green is directly across from red and next to yellow.

Orange and yellow are sunny colors, very suitable for a dining area although, naturally, many other color combinations are possible. This chapter tells all about color, its function, and what works and what doesn't. The color wheel at right will help you.

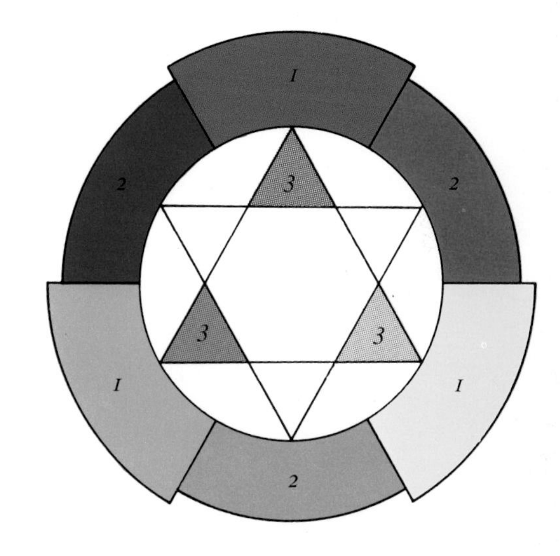

1. The primary colors; red, yellow, and blue
2. The secondary colors; mixtures of red and yellow (orange), yellow and blue (green), blue and red (violet)
3. The tertiary colors; mixtures of 1 and 2

Complementary colors
These are the primary and secondary colors that lie across from each other, such as red and green, yellow and violet, and orange and blue.

Tertiary colors
When the colors next to each other are mixed, we get the tertiary colors: yellow-orange comes from yellow and orange; red and violet make crimson; and so forth. These tertiary colors have a somewhat muted character, but are often the most pleasant colors we can use in our homes because of their soft nature.

Understanding colors
To make up your own color combinations it is necessary, and not difficult, to understand color. There are, for example, a large number of shades of blue, red, and yellow.The difference between light and dark is not difficult to understand. With practice you can learn the differences between, for example, yellow green, moss green, blue green, and gray green. The same is true for the many shades of white. Once you really understand color you will see the differences between blue white, gray white, green white, and yellow white. If you put gray white next to yellow white, for instance, both colors seem stronger.

The character of the colors
Colors have a great influence on shape. Warm colors enlarge, cool colors reduce the size of an object. Colors containing red and yellow, such as red-orange, yellow-red, and red are warm colors. Colors containing blue are cool. Green is a neutral color; it neither enlarges nor reduces. Green can be either warm or cold.
If you crochet a shape in yellow and the same shape in blue, the yellow shape will look larger than the blue.

The color and the yarn
Wool gives a warmer, deeper look to color than, for instance, cotton. Cotton colors appear sharper than the same colors in wool.

The combination of colors
Complementary colors combine well as both have the same color values of hardness, softness, darkness, and so forth.
With a basic color in various shades from light to dark use a complementary color with the same shades.

Red
Red is warm, stimulating, and advances. It stimulates activity and in a modern interior with little sun or other light red is exciting.
Red's secondary and tertiary colors, such as orange-red, give a warm, vivid, clear effect. They require thought to work with properly. In crochet, yellow and white are excellent contrast colors with red.

Red and green
Red alone is somewhat obtrusive; used with green it becomes more balanced.
This combination is suitable for a child's room or an eat-in kitchen provided brown or white furniture or other objects are used.

Green
This is a popular color for interiors. Green rests the eyes. In addition to the secondary color, there are many shades of green.
Good combinations with green are red, white, black, and brown.
Green's other versions, such as yellow-green, are sunny and friendly and restful in busy areas such as the kitchen and the playroom and children's room. A combination of blue and green is even cooler and still more peaceful and suitable, therefore, for a bedroom or study. For contrast, red-orange, white, and brown are excellent.

Yellow
An uncomplicated color, peppy and cheerful, that works well with light furniture. Yellow is the symbol of sunlight and comes in many shades.
The combination of yellow with orange is radiant, lively, and suitable for kitchens, eating areas, and work rooms. Good contrast colors for yellow are white and rose. If the yellow seems too strong, violet,

This stitch is made up of single crochets which are worked from left to right.

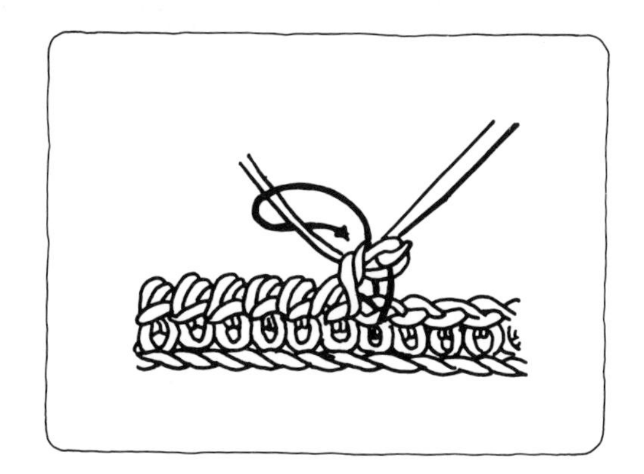

Arches of chains accented with single crochet and picots.

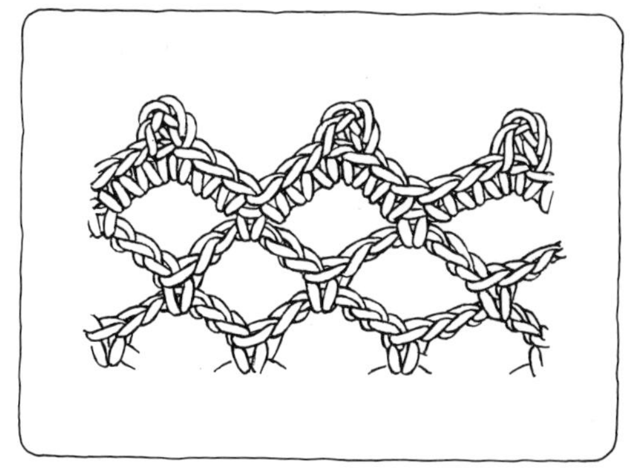

white, or black can be used as the accents to tone it down.

Blue

Color, restful, and elegant. A relaxing color and therefore suitable for bedrooms. The contrast colors for blue are white, brown, and orange-red.

Orange with blue offers two contrasts as you have warm and cool colors used together. Shades of these colors can be very beautiful in combination.

Explore for yourself

Take a paint box or a box of crayons and combine various colors with each other. Avoid using too much of one color or too little of another color in planning something you will make. Once you have worked out the colors you want to use in your crochet, make a sample crochet section using the different colors to find the combinations that are best for your eating area or kitchen.

Keep the knowledge of color you have just acquired clearly in your mind and you will certainly succeed in working out a good combination.

Let's look at the *cushion* on the bench more closely. It has on it a crocheted work of orange with yellow and green crocheted chains as contrast. On the table there is a *placemat* which is crocheted in stripes, also with orange as the main color. Crochet a chain of stitches with a double thread of cotton 13 inches long. On this crochet in single crochet $\frac{3}{4}$ inch brown, $1\frac{1}{2}$ inches green, $\frac{3}{4}$ inch yellow, 8 inches orange, followed by the stripes in reverse (that is, yellow, green, brown).

Another possible color combination might be to have the main color in green with the other colors orange-red, brown, and very light green. Or perhaps you would prefer apple green as the main color with dark green, orange, and brown providing the contrast.

The table mats

These are crocheted in shades of one color. The center is a light shade which becomes dark as it moves to the outside.

How to: Using the light color crochet a chain of 4 stitches and close this with a slip stitch into a ring. Crochet 8 single crochets in the ring, crocheting one chain as the first single crochet. Close each round with a slip stitch in the first stitch. In the following row increase at regular intervals so that the crochet stays flat. Pick up both loops of the stitches when crocheting. When the diameter of the circle is $4\frac{1}{2}$ inches finish off the light colored yarn. Continue to work with the next shade. Attach it at the back of the previous round and crochet half double crochet stitches in this round. The last row of the light color is a chain around the work. Continue to increase in a regular way. Work 3 double crochet in back on the last row in the stitches beneath. Then crochet a popcorn row as follows: *5 double crochet, 1 popcorn which is 5 double crochets in the same stitch. Take the crochet hook out of the stitch and put through the top of the first double crochet and then through the loop of the fifth

This round rug is crocheted in rug yarn and, as accents, has two rows of popcorn stitches. You can decide yourself how big you want such a rug to be and simply crochet around until you have the size.
The table runner is worked in a combination of single crochet and half double crochet in stripes of shades of red and green.

double crochet. Wrap the yarn around the hook and pull this through both loops on the needle. Repeat from *while continuing to increase. Crochet 1 row of single crochet on this popcorn row. Continue crocheting with the third color: 1 row double crochet, working the first row at the back 1 row lower. Crochet as a finishing row 1 round of single crochet from left to right as illustrated on page 31.

Crocheted lamp shade
Before we leave the dining area let's look at the lamp over the dining table. It is a cover that can be used with many shades. The top is pulled in by a crocheted cord. The crochet work runs along the bottom ring of the frame to the inside and then up by about $1\frac{1}{2}$ inches where this edge is held by a thin elastic. Along the bottom, points of scallops are crocheted to which beads are attached.
The colors of the crochet run from light to dark with a lining under the crochet of a complementary color so that the pattern of the crochet stands out.
Begin at the bottom and work a chain making it, for instance, 10 times the number of bars the frame has. Close the chain into a ring. Crochet on this *1 double crochet, 2 chains, skip 2 chains, and repeat from.* The cord will later be drawn through this round. Crochet in the following row *2 double crochet, 2 chain, and 2 double crochets on 1 double crochet of the previous row, 3 chain and crochet a single crochet in the following double crochet, 3 chain, repeat from*. Crochet the following row on

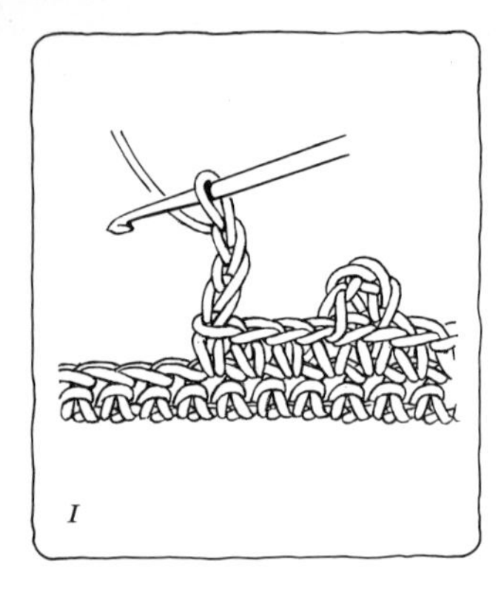

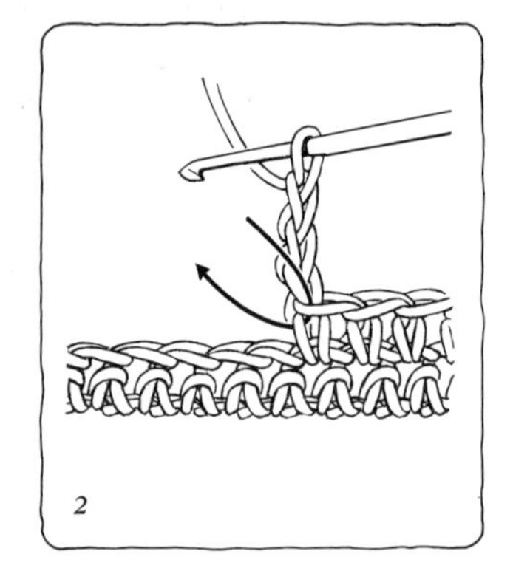

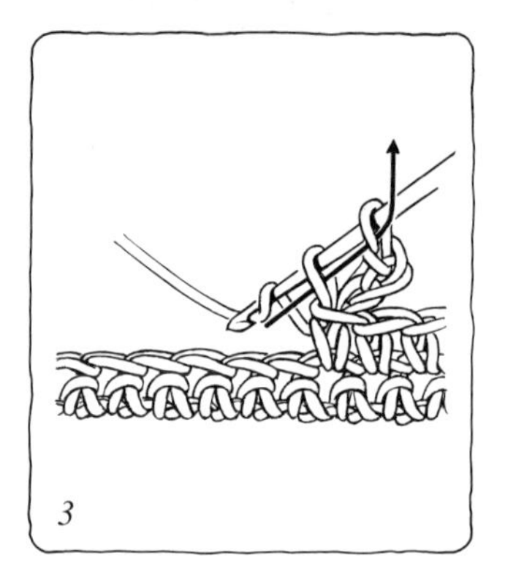

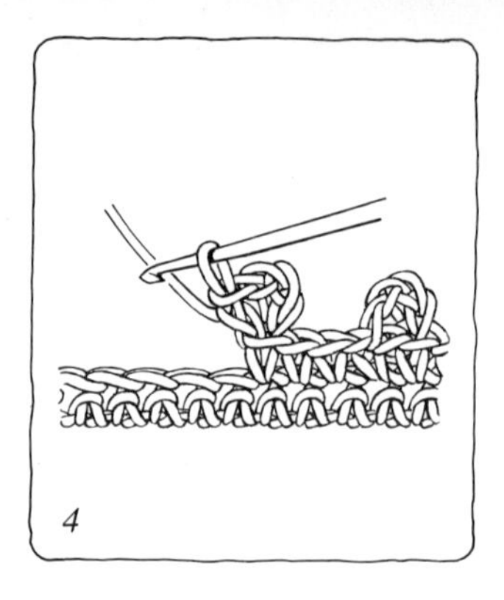

An edging that alternates single crochet with picots.

the 2 chains between the double crochet, again 2 double crochet with the 2 chains and 2 double crochet, and crochet 3 chains, 1 single crochet on the 3rd chain arch of the previous row with then, again, 3 chains. Close every round with a slip stitch. In the following row always work double crochets on the 2 chains between the double crochets and between these chains and single crochet on every chain arch until the right width is reached.

You may possibly crochet more than 3 chains between the single crochets. There must not be more than 3 arches between the double crochet groups. Crochet double crochet above double crochet but in the middle arch between the groups of double crochet work 2 double crochet with 2 chains and 2 double crochet. Crochet chains between every group of double crochets, as many as are necessary for the width you need; this can, for example, be 5 or more. Change the color when your lamp shade cover is one third of its height. Crochet to the bottom border and change the color once again. For the bottom, crochet a further 1½ inches in arches, and end. Crochet some rows of scallops or points at the underside and sew between these some beads.

Points can be crocheted by working 2 additional double crochet on the middle chain in every following row.

From table mat to floor covering

Use for your material a heavy yarn, such as a heavy rug yarn, and a large crochet hook. The rug which is shown is one where the colors do not, as in the table mats, go from light to dark but rather are chosen to make a dark brown background with two lighter colored rows of popcorn stitches. There are many warm colors that work well with brown. Brown comes from a mixture of black and orange and fits into almost every room. It is a very useful color. If we used green borders on this rug it would look somber and dull. Red and gray could be used successfully or a background of dark green with gold and red. You could, of course, have the background color light and the band of popcorn stitch dark – it depends entirely on the floor on which the rug will be placed. If the interior or the floor is complete and doesn't ask for a rug, make the rug in one color. This rug is not made, as in the case of the table mats, with single crochet but with double crochet. In crocheting the background don't close the row as in the case of the table mats, but crochet in spiral fashion. When you are closing the popcorn section it is a good idea to include a colored thread at the beginning of the round so that you will know where it began.

How to: crochet a chain of 6 stitches and close it with a slip stitch into a ring. Crochet 11 half double crochets in the ring and crochet 2 half double crochet in every half double crochet in order to increase in the next row. In the next row increase by another 11 half double crochets, by crocheting 2 half double crochets in every 2nd half double crochet. In the following row crochet 2 half double crochets in every 3rd half double crochet, and so forth. Be sure the rug stays flat during the crocheting, if not

skip a couple of the increases in the next row. Crochet about 23 rows to the first popcorn border. For the standing border, crochet 1 round of double crochets made with the hook brought from back to front to make the double crochet from right to left. Do not increase when working these. If you plan to crochet the popcorn border in a different color, then crochet this row, too, with the new color. Close the row with a slip stitch and begin the next row with 2 chains. Crochet 2 rows of half double crochet and 1 row of double crochet worked from right to left as above. The following row, *the popcorn row:*
* 11 double crochet, crochet 1 popcorn of 5 double crochet, that is work 5 double crochet in 1 stitch, take the hook out of the last double crochet, put the hook through the bottom of the first double crochet and pull the loop of the 5th double crochet through the 1st double crochet, repeat from *. Increase as needed between the popcorn stitches. After this popcorn row repeat the same rows as you did earlier, that is double crochet behind double crochet, working again with the background color. Crochet 3 rows of half double crochet and then a 2nd popcorn border. Continue to work in this way, making more popcorn borders if you wish or, if you like it better, more double crochet rows between the popcorn rows. When you have reached the right size, finish the edge with a row of single crochet from left to right as shown on page 31.

The runner

The simple table runner is crocheted in a pattern that can be used for many purposes including placemats. The stripes are made of the complementary colors green and red. The stripes change in width from 2 to 4 to 6 to 8 to 10 rows and then back again from 8 to 6 to 4 to 2 rows with the five colors in the same order. If you want the same effect have the color shades move from light to dark, for example, from gold to red-brown and from dark green to blue-green.

The pattern

Crochet an uneven number of chain stitches. *1st row:* 1 half double crochet in the 3rd stitch from the hook, * skip one chain and crochet in the following stitch: 1 single crochet and 1 half double crochet, repeat from *. *2nd row:* 1 chain to turn and crochet in every single crochet of the previous row: 1 single crochet and 1 half double crochet. Repeat after the 2nd row.

Other color combinations

Consider light rose, dark rose, purple, very dark purple, and dark beige or shades of green and blue with a very light yellow or gold.

Open scallops, used for the lamp; crochet 2 double crochet, 2 chains, and 2 double crochets in 1 stitch.

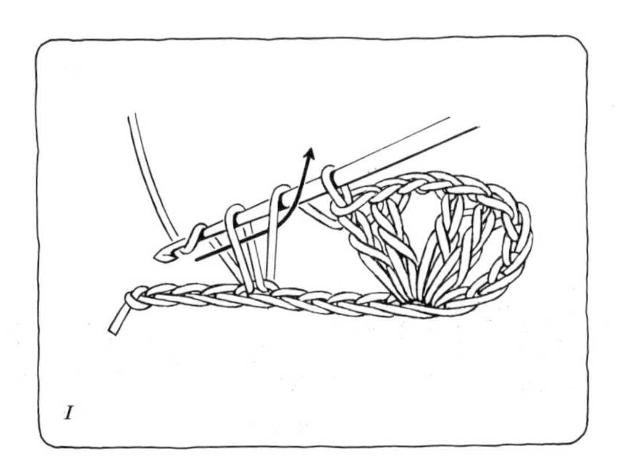

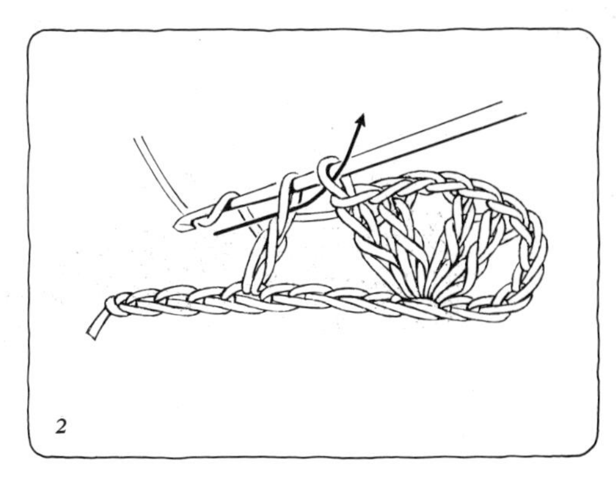

4 Cotton in the Kitchen

Checked gingham is always popular in the kitchen. A crocheted insertion in the fabric color with a ruffled border below decorates the kitchen window attractively. On page 40 you can find other color combinations and another design for insertion lace. The pattern for this one is on page 39.

'My kitchen is my pride' European grandmothers embroidered on their kitchen towels. They were truly proud of their kitchens which were spic and span, cozy and comfortable. Since those days many things have changed. The old fashioned pump has been replaced by running water, the time consuming coal stove by a handy gas or electric range. All the modern household apliances have made things somewhat easier for us but our kitchens have lost a good deal of their coziness through these appliances and have come to appear somewhat sterile and cold. Fortunately newer houses and apartments are being build with more eat-in kitchens and open kitchens and manufacturers are offering us our appliances in more choice of cheerful colors. There are all kinds of decorations which we can buy for our kitchen walls and a good deal of thought has been given to the way kitchen items look. Whether your kitchen is small or large it is your kitchen and it can certainly benefit from being made cozier and more liveable.

The valance

The technique of filet crochet was described in the chapter on crocheting curtains. This valance is crocheted in filet crochet with the points created by increasing and then decreasing 1 block on a side in every row. The fringe at the bottom of the valance is made from 6 strands which are knotted. The chart shows how the motifs must be worked in the filet crochet or try your own hand at designing a motif that is suitable for crochet.

From valance to table cloth or spread

By repeating the motif on the chart in a long strip and then joining strips together with crochet you can make a crocheted spread or table cloth. Because the design is an open one it can be very effective worked in colored thread or yarn with a contrasting

Below right. Here is a valance worked in filet crochet with a fringed edging. The pattern for this is on the next page.

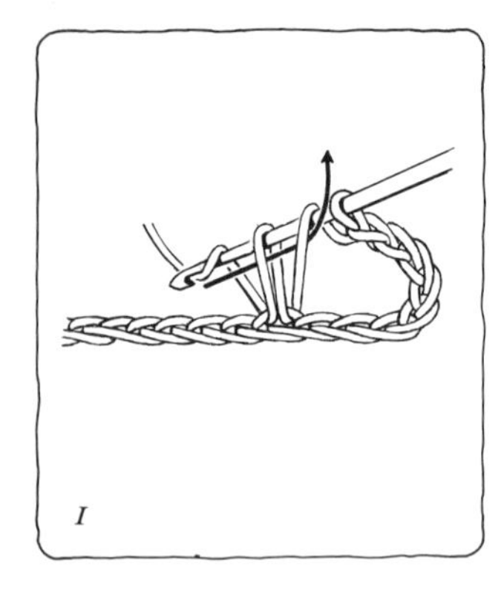

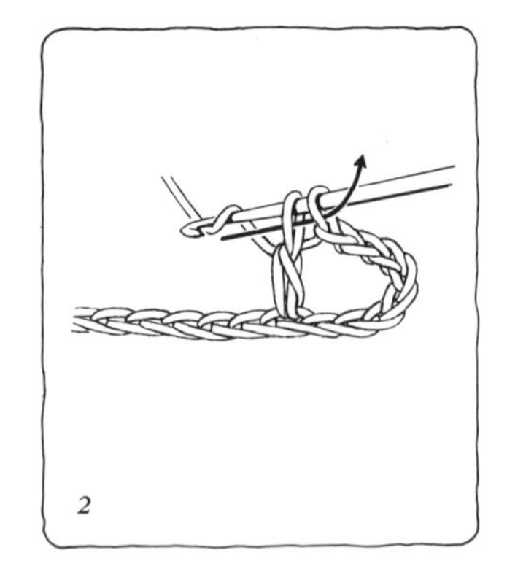

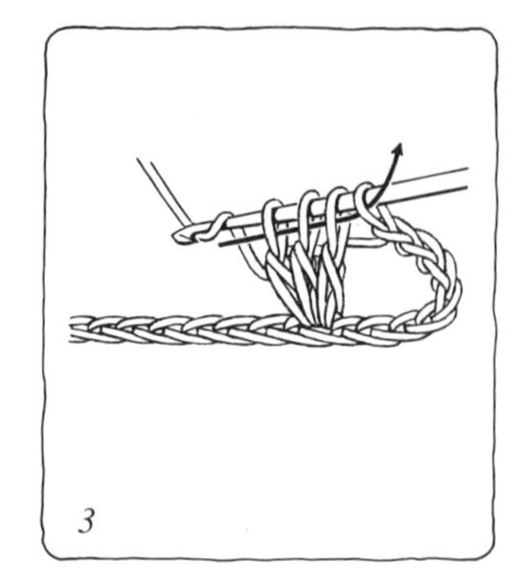

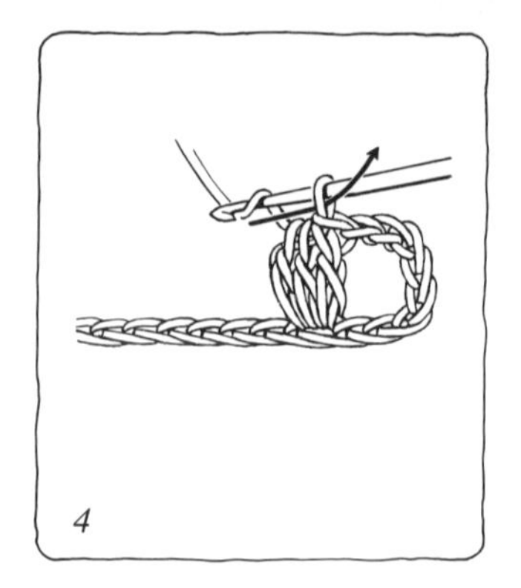

Here is how cluster stitch is worked. You can see it in the picture on page 41.

This is the pattern of the valance which is made in filet crochet. See also page 10.

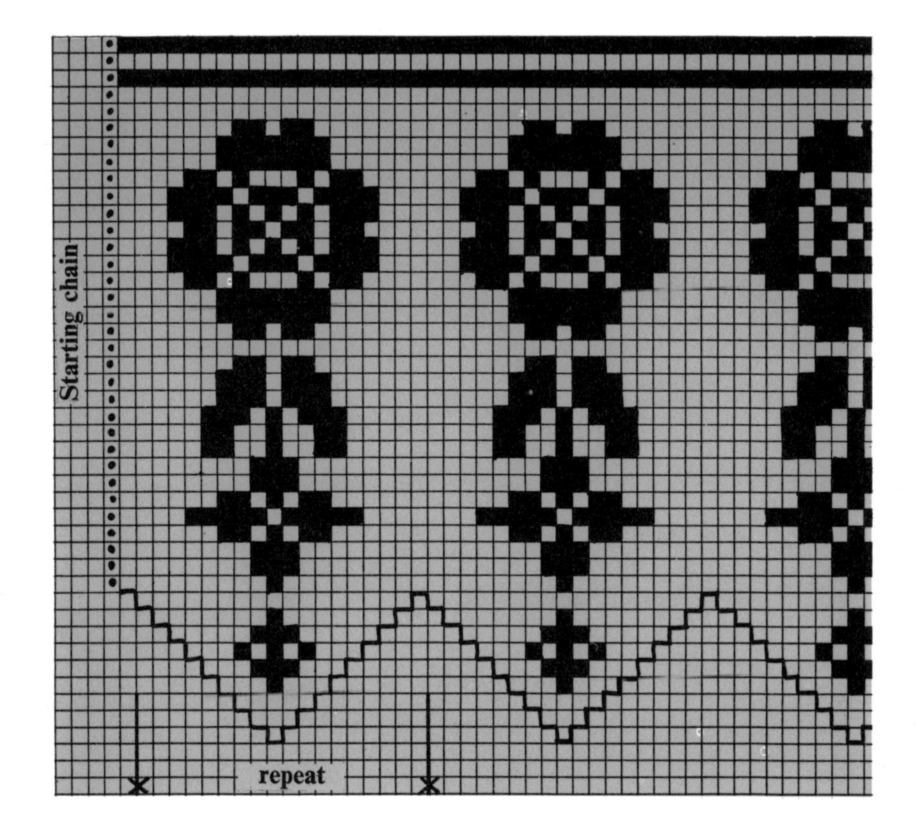

cloth placed underneath. The pointed design can be worked all around the edge, with or without the motif as part of it.

Insertion

The name, insertion, says it all. Insertions were much used in the past for bed clothes. Long before the groom was in sight, the daughters of a family would be working hard on their linen trousseaus. This was not only embroidered but additionally embellished with crochet designs. The insertion was used at the top of the sheets and decorated with flower motifs, sayings, and so forth. This crochet method is simple which means people of any age and experience can get good results with it.

Insertions in the kitchen are worked into a window curtain. Checked gingham or another curtain fabric can be used to dress up the window of the kitchen. Many different colors and types of curtain fabrics are available in the stores and the true handwork fabrics can also be good for curtains. A suitable kind of crochet thread for working an insertion in a cotton or partly linen fabric is, naturally, one that isn't too thick. The small balls of perle yarn, for instance, are good. There are also many dramatic yarns that are suitable for this purposes including some with little flecks that work especially well on a rather rough cotton.

The number of chain stitches for an insertion depends on the kind of filet crochet you plan to make. Every opening is one block that can be made from 1 double crochet with 2 chains or 1 half double crochet with 1 chain. If you choose the first, then you need 3 chains for one block. With the second, you need 1 chain. In order to make the first block you must chain an extra 5 stitches after the chain row. Begin, then, the 1st row after the chain with a double crochet in the 9th stitch from the crochet hook. In the case of blocks made of 1 double crochet and 1 chain you'll need 2 chains for each block at the beginning plus, for turning, 1 chain and 4 chains extra. Begin in this case at the 7th chain from the hook in the 1st row. On pages 38 en 39 are some charts of designs that can be used in the kitchen but try to design something yourself. A design you have worked out yourself is always more satisfactory than one designed by someone else.

Inserting the crochet

Begin by making a narrow seam on the back of the top of the curtain and sew the crochet work to this smoothly. From the remaining fabric cut a strip 3 times the width of the curtain, and baste a narrow hem along the long side of it. Gather this then to the right width for the curtain and sew this ruffle to the bottom of the crochet insertion. Make the remaining hems in the fabric.

Such an insertion can also be used in a tea cozy – sew the insertion at the bottom of the cozy – or one or two such insertions can be used in a linen cloth. Keep in mind the importance of using the right crochet yarn for the fabric.

Cabinets

Let us go on to kitchen cabinets. The cabinet shelves can be decorated with small crocheted edgings. If the cabinet just holds dishes, choose for your crochet yarn or thread a color that picks up the colors on the dishes. If the cabinet is more of a junk cabinet, or if you have objects in many different colors in it, then choose white for your edgings.

Cotton is the most suitable fiber for the yarn as it can be washed easily. The edgings pictured are narrow and simple to crochet.

Scalloped edging

This is crocheted on the diagonal. To begin, crochet a chain of 9 stitches.

1st row: chain 4, work 1 single crochet in the 5th chain from the hook, chain 5, skip 3 chains, and crochet 1 single crochet in the last stitch.

2nd row: chain 5, work 1 single crochet on the arch, chain 5, work 1 single crochet on the next arch, chain 5 and work 1 single crochet in the last arch.

3rd row: chain 5 to turn, work 1 single crochet in the first arch, chain 5, work

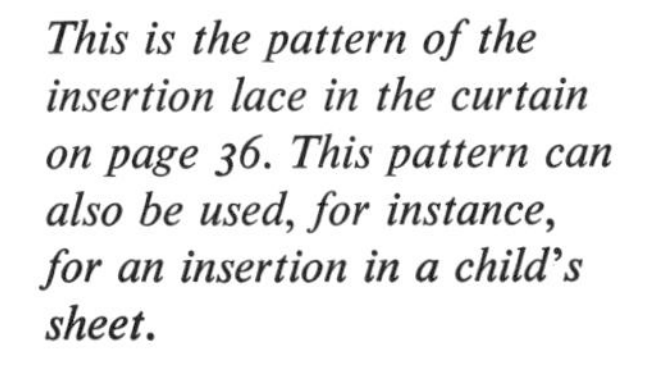

This is the pattern of the insertion lace in the curtain on page 36. This pattern can also be used, for instance, for an insertion in a child's sheet.

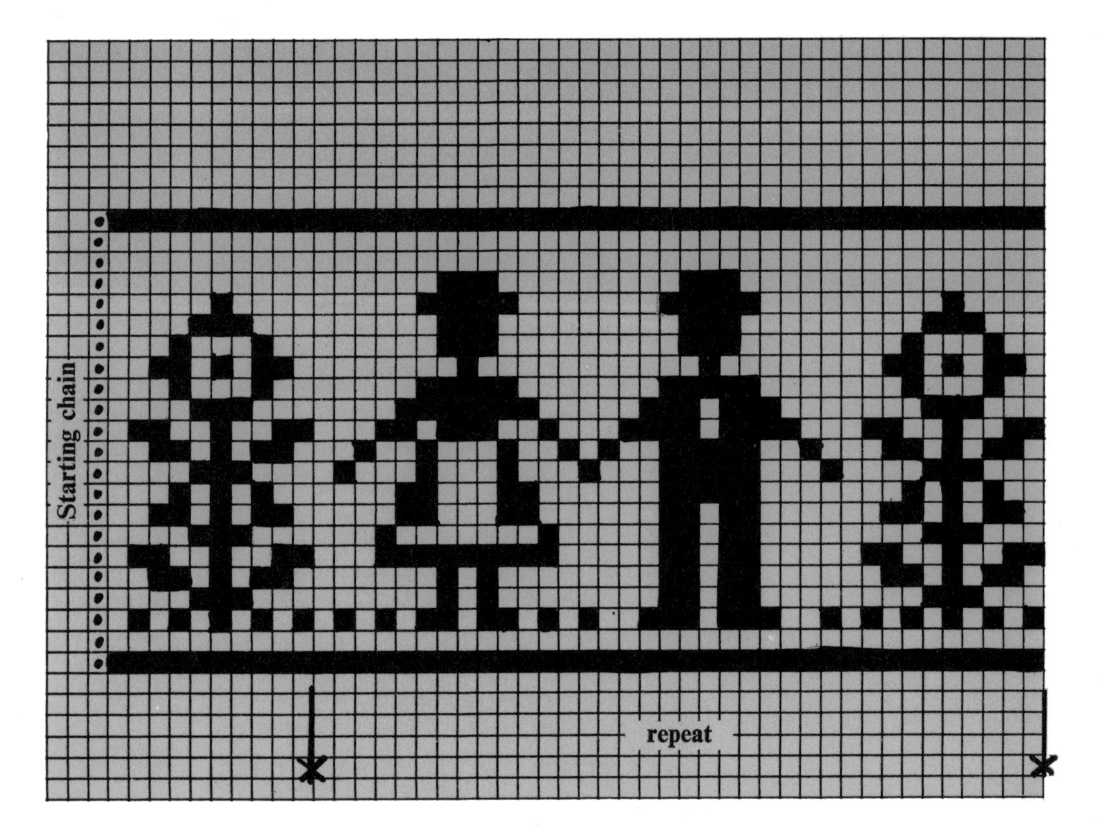

This curtain, like the curtain on page 36, has a crocheted insertion in the same color as the gingham. You can find the pattern on page 43.

1 single crochet in the following arch, chain 5 and work 1 single crochet in the last arch.
4th row: work 4 chains, crochet 4 double crochet in the following arch, chain 1, work 4 double crochet in the following arch, chain 1, work 8 double crochet on the 5 arches of the 3rd row, work 1 single crochet on the arch of the 1st row.
5th row: chain 3, skip 1 double crochet, crochet 1 single crochet in the following double crochet, work 3 chains, skip 1 double crochet, work 1 single crochet, chain 3, skip 1 double crochet, work 1 single crochet in the following double crochet (this is the last double crochet of the group of 8 double crochet), work 5 chains, work 1 single crochet in the chain of the previous row, work 5 chains, work 1 chain in the following chain to turn. Repeat from the 2nd row until the edging reaches the desired length.

This same edging can be used as a finishing touch to a cloth or placemat worked in single or double crochet. If it is worked with a thin thread and a steel crochet hook, it can be used around a handkerchief.
Narrow edgings are always worthwhile for finishing the items you make.

Pointed edging
This edging is also worked on the diagonal. Start by crocheting a chain of 4 stitches.
1st row: crochet 2 double crochet in the 4th chain from the hook, chain 2, work 3 double crochet. Turn with 3 chains.
2nd row: Crochet on the chain between the group of double crochets: 3 double crochet, 2 chains, and 3 double crochet, then work 2 chains and 1 double crochet on the last double crochet of this group.
3rd row: work 3 chains as the 1st double crochet, then 2 chains, then 1 double crochet on the 1st double crochet, 2 chains, crochet on the chains between the group: 3 double crochet with 2 chains and 3 double crochets. Turn with 3 chains.
4th row: crochet on the chains between the group: 3 double crochet, 2 chains, and 3 double crochet, then 2 chains and crochet 1 double crochet in the last double crochet of this group, 2 chains, 1 double crochet in the next double crochet, 2 chains, and 1 double crochet in the last double crochet.
5th row: crochet 3 chains for the 1st double crochet, 2 chains, 1 double crochet in the double crochet, 2 chains, 1 double crochet in the 1st double crochet of the group, 2 chains, crochet in the chains of the group: 3 double crochet with 2 chains and 3 double crochets. Repeat these last 4 rows.

Finishing: End the last row at the top. Crochet along the entire border * chain 5,

Top right; a kitchen towel crocheted in many colors. Instructions for making these squares are on the next page.

The instructions for these shelf edgings can be found on the page on the left: the instructions for the oven mitt are on page 43. The wide border can be used in many ways. Work out your own design if you prefer: this one is a variation on the insertion used in the green and white checked gingham curtain.

1 single crochet in the 3 chains to turn, repeat from *. Crochet along the points: 1 single crochet, 1 picot (3 chains and 1 slip stitch in the 1st chain), 1 single crochet in the double crochet, crochet at the point: 1 single crochet, 1 picot, 2 single crochet, 1 picot, 2 single crochet, 1 picot and 1 single crochet so there are 3 picots at the point. This edging can also be used to finish another article.

Border with cluster stitches

On page 38 you can see how cluster stitches are made. Begin with a chain of stitches as long as the shelf you are decorating is wide. Crochet 4 extra chains for turning.

1st row: begin in the 7th chain from the hook with 1 single crochet, * chain 7, skip 5 chains, 1 single crochet in the following chain, repeat from *. The following 2 rows are arches * chain 7, work 1 single crochet in the following arch, repeat from *.

4th row: * 5 chains, crochet in the 4th chain of the arch: 3 cluster stitches with 5 chains and then 3 cluster stitches, then 5 chains

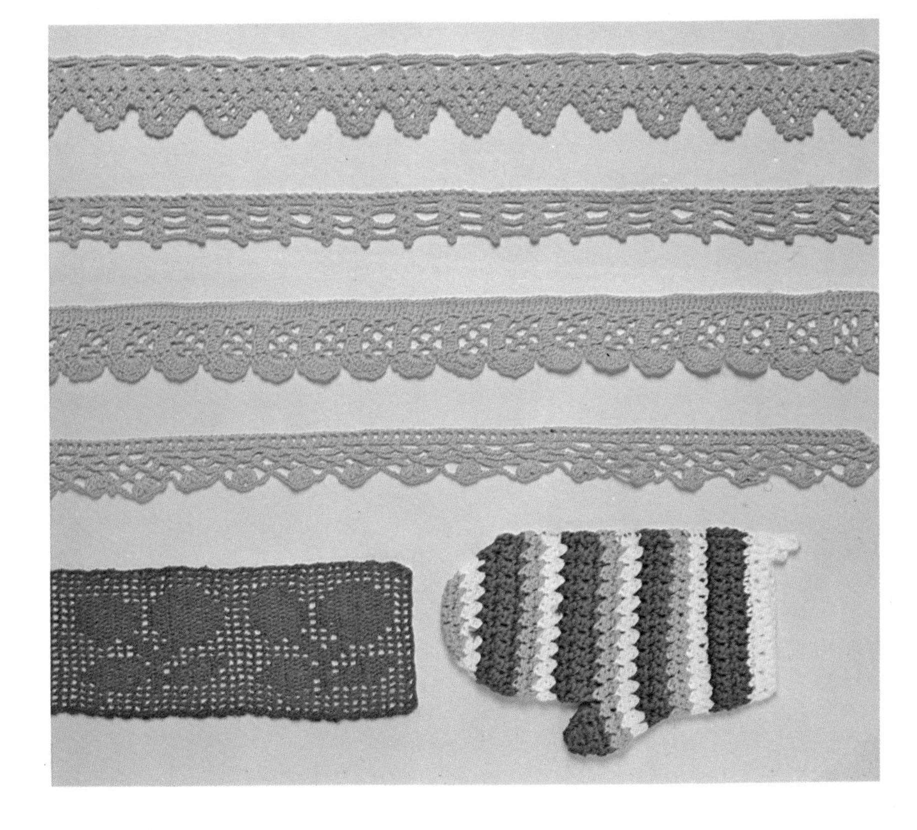

and 1 single crochet in the following arch, and 1 single crochet in the following arch

Finishing: crochet along the top of the edging one row of alternately 1 double crochet and 1 chain, skipping 1 stitch of the chain.

Trellis work border

This is a splendid looking edging for your cabinets. The stitch is the same as that used for the lamp over the table so, if you want to make both, you have instant coordination. Begin with a chain of stitches and crochet on this one row, alternating 1 double crochet and 1 chain, and skipping 1 chain.

Following row: turn with 4 chains, work 1 double crochet in the first double crochet, * chain 5, skip 5 double crochet and crochet on the following stitch: 2 double crochet with 2 chains and 2 double crochet, repeat from *. Finish with 1 double crochet, 1 chain, and 1 double crochet in the last stitch. Turn with 4 chains.

Following row: crochet 1 double crochet in the double crochet of the side, chain 5, and

crochet in the middle of the group of double crochets in the chains 2 double crochet with 2 chains and 2 double crochet. Finish the row with 1 double crochet, 1 chain, and 1 double crochet.
When you feel that the edging is wide enough, finish it off. If you want it wider, repeat the last row.

This border is also suitable for curtains.
By repeating this design over and over you can make a long curtain. For the last row crochet instead of the 2 chains between the group of double crochet a picot of 3 chains with 1 slip stitch in the 1st chain.
With these four examples of borders and your own imagination you are sure to be able to work out borders for your own kitchen cabinets that will make you proud every time you open the door.

Hand towel
Designs which are crocheted in squares have been in the past and still are today extremely popular. An example is the hand towel on page 41, which has been crocheted in a granny square design.
Don't worry about working out a color scheme for such kitchen items as hand towels, pot holders, and so forth. The combination of different colors, used with white, such as the picture shows requires less thought and, for a kitchen with many colors, is a better choice.

Crocheting squares
Begin with a chain of 3 stitches and close this into a ring with a slip stitch. Continue to crochet around; begin every row with 3 chains for the first double crochet and close every round with a slip stitch in the 3rd chain from the beginning.
1st row: crochet 3 double crochets with 2 chains, repeat 3 more times. The 2 arches will form the corners of the squares. In each arch crochet: 3 double crochets, 2 chains, and 3 double crochets, crochet 2 chains between these groups for the side 2 chains.
In the following row crochet in the corner arches again 3 double crochet, 2 chains, and 3 double crochet and in the arches of the side crochet 3 double crochets. Now, between the double crochet group and the sides crochet 1 chain. Repeat these last rows until the square is the desired size.
Every row can be crocheted in a different color. To change colors, work the last of the section in the old color with the new color. If you crochet the square larger it can serve as a pot holder but, since this crochet work has holes between the double crochet stitches, the pot holder must be lined with a square of the same size crocheted in single crochet to protect the hand from the heat. Place both these sections together and crochet around the edges with a row of single crochets and picots. At the end of the last row crochet a chain for hanging up the pot holder in your kitchen.

Crocheted patchwork
Colorful patchwork designs can be made by using, in place of pieces of fabric, squares you have crocheted. The colorful towel shown in this chapter is an example. If you use wool or a warm synthetic yarn such as acrylic instead of cotton and add 2 or 3 rows to every square, your crochet can grow into a blanket or spread. The choice of colors here is very important. For a children's room the colors can be light and peppy. If the patchwork is destined for the living room or another quiet spot, choose quieter colors. Think also of a black and white combination with here and there a touch of light green or violet. The same color scheme and design could also be used for pillow covers.
In the kitchen, of course, your patchwork square designs should be made of cotton, as it can be easily washed. Here, too, consider making pillow covers.

Oven mitts
These must have a thick, heavy structure. Cotton is the best yarn; don't use wool or a synthetic. Crochet with a double thread, making stripes if you want. The mitt consists of a front and back side. Crochet a chain of 23 stitches.
1st row: crochet 1 half double crochet in

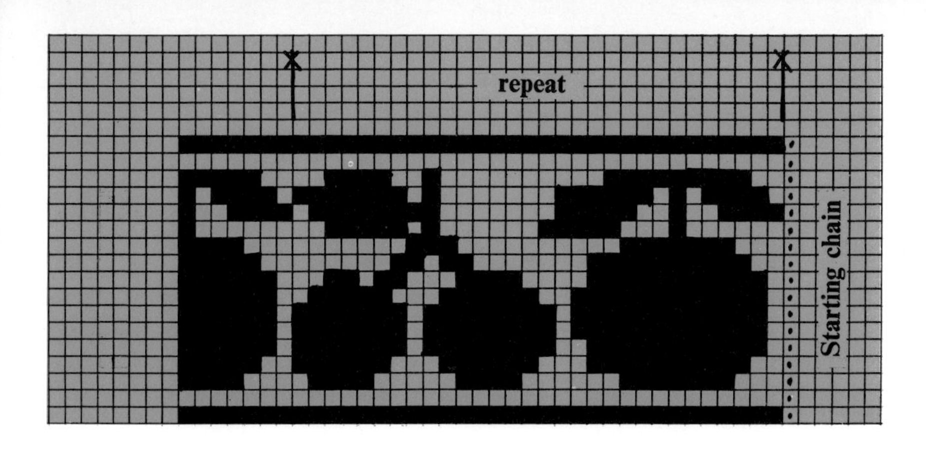

This fruit pattern can be used for an insertion in a curtain or, if made of somewhat thicker yarns, as a decorative edging on, for instance, a mantel.

the 3rd chain from the crochet hook, * skip 1 chain and crochet in the following stitch: 1 single crochet with 1 half double crochet, repeat from *.
2nd and all following rows: work 1 chain for turning, crochet in every single crochet: 1 single crochet and 1 half double crochet (this is 1 pattern). Each row has, therefore, 11 of this pattern. Increase in the 8th and 9th row and in the 14th and 15th row by 1 stitch on the left side. This makes 13 patterns. After the 16th row from the beginning crochet 10 patterns on the right side of the work; the remaining 2 patterns are for the thumb. Crochet 10 rows further in these 10 patterns then, for the rounding of the top, decrease by 1 stitch at the beginning and end of the next 6 rows. When there are 4 pattern sections remaining, finish off.

To make the thumb, attach the yarn in the 10th pattern at the 17th row and crochet on the 2 remaining patterns. After the 1st row decrease by 1 stitch on each side, do the same in the following row and fasten off. Crochet the back of the mitt in reverse. Sew both parts together and crochet along the edge where you began 1 row of single crochet and 2 rows in the pattern. At the end of the last row work a chain loop so the mitt can be hung up. With this pattern as a base, you can make many variations of this mitt in color and stitches. The width of the starting row should be about $4\frac{3}{4}$ inches for each section.

Other Decorations

There are many other places in your kitchen such as the window sill or, if you are lucky enough to have a fireplace, the mantel, which can be decorated along the edge with filet crochet, for instance.
Rows of stitches which are worked back and forth in double crochet in two colors, as in the squares on the towel, give crochet the effect of panes of stained glass. Crochet, changing 1 row of light for 1 row of dark: 3 double crochet next to each other with 3 chain between each group. In the following rows crochet chains above the double crochet and 3 double crochet in the chains. On these pages only a few suggestions of colors to use in the kitchen have been given. Don't, of course, forget among these color suggestions the traditional red and white.

5 Decorative Room Dividers

In every corner there is some spot that's right for a decoration such as this. It is a room divider but could also be used, for instance, to hide shelves. This is crocheted with the fingers only and is easy enough for children to do.

Probably the oldest form of crochet is crocheting using just the fingers. The tip of the pointer finger serves as the hook of the crochet hook. Using this method you can work a crocheted cord that can be quite impressive. This method of crochet is simple enough for children to learn and can provide a good way for them to pass away time on a car, train, or plane.

Finger Crochet

If you want to teach a child how to crochet in this way, here is how to do it. Start the child with a not-too-thin thread, using, if need be, thin string. Start as in the same way for starting a crochet chain; see illustration A on the next page. Slide this loop onto the pointer of the right hand. Hold the end between the thumb and pointer of your left hand. With the tip of your right pointer, take the other end of thread and pull it through the loop on your finger. The first chain stitch has now been worked. By continuing to do this you will get a long chain of stitches. These may be quite large at the start. If you continually pull each crocheted chain tight, the chain will become firmer and the chains smaller. See the illustration on page 46. Once the child understands finger crocheting you can introduce crocheting the chain in two colors. Take contrasting colors. Make a loop to start with the darker of the two colors and make the first stitch with the light color, the next stitch with the dark, the next light, and so forth. See illustration C on page 46. If the thread is not as thick as you want it to be, use three strands or more depending on the thickness you want. If the finished cord has been crocheted loosely, a row of slip stitches can be worked along it, again just using the fingers. To do this, put the right pointer through 1 loop of the bottom stitch of the chain and pull the thread through both loops with the finger, then push the tip of the right pointer through 1 loop of the next stitch and again pull the thread through both the loops. Continue in this way until you reach the end of the cord.

A variation on the divider on the left hand page. This one has beads crocheted into it (see also page 47).

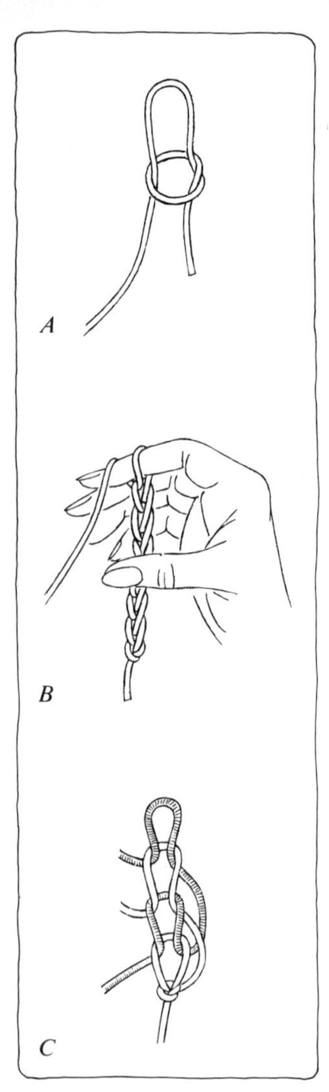

A. B. C. Crocheting with the fingers.

D. Finger crochet with a single thread.

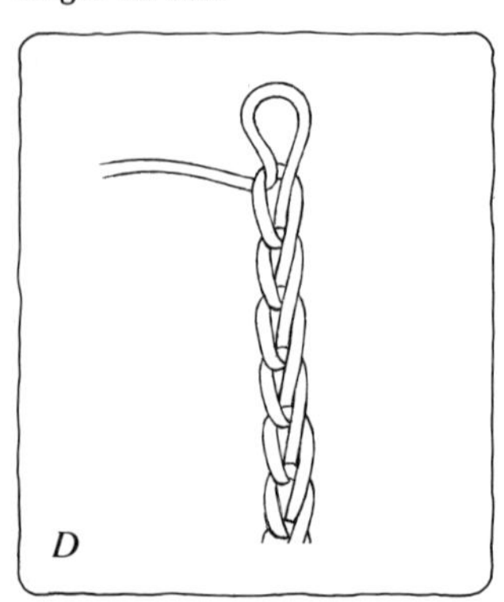

This makes the entire chain both stronger and thicker.

Knotted braid

Another way to make a chain without using a crochet hook is by knotting a braid.
Tie the start of your thread to something like the handle of the door. Make a loop about 1¼ inches long as close as possible to where you have attached your thread. Hold the loop tightly between your left thumb and forefinger.
Push the pointer of your right hand through the loop, pick up the thread with the tip of this finger and, in loop form, pull the thread through the first loop. Now push your pointer through the loop you've just made and pull another loop through. These loops can be pulled tight very easily; see illustration D.
To work a cord of this type you will need a thread or yarn which is about 5 times the length you want the finished cord.

A Two-Thread Knotted Cord

Tie 2 threads to something such as the handle of a door. Hold one thread in your left hand and one thread in your right hand. Make a loop as close as possible to the point where the thread is attached using the thread in your left hand. Push the pointer of your right hand through the loop and pick up the thread from your right hand, holding the first loop tightly between your thumb and middle finger. Pull the left thread through the last loop with your left pointer and drop the loop formed with the right pointer. Pull the loop until it is very tight. Continue in this way alternating the right and left threads. This makes a very firm cord which can be used, for instance, to finish an edge. See drawing E.

Room divider

The room divider illustrated has been crocheted with 4 strands of yarn. Use 3 strands in a basic color and 1 strand in a shade of the basic color. Use a different shade for each cord to add to the subtle effect. Crochet a chain with a medium sized crochet hook about 87 inches long. Knot the cord at random, keeping the spaces between the knots between 3 and 4 inches. Occasionally vary this by making two knots very close together.

Finishing

The crocheted cords can be attached to your ceiling or doorway or window in various ways. You can sew them to cotton tape about 1 inch wide, for instance, and then sew rings at the top of this tape. Add a rod and you can hang the curtain on the rod.

Crocheting a border at the top

To do this, crochet a chain using 4 strands of yarn, making the chain the width of your room divider. On top of this crochet chain stitch arches: 5 chain stitch, skip 3 stitches of the chain, crochet in the following chain 1 single crochet, and so on until you have come to the end of the chain. Continue to crochet arches of 5 chain stitches in the following rows and in each arch of the previous row work 1 single crochet. Crochet until the border measures about 4 inches wide. Knot or sew the cords to the bottom row of arches, skipping arches when necessary to space the cords as you want.

Divider with beads

For this work use a fairly thick thread and thread onto it the number of beads you plan to use for one cord. Crochet a chain, working a bead into it every 2½ to 4 inches. Slide the bead against the last crocheted stitch, wind the cotton around the hook, and pull it through behind the bead. See illustrations F1 and F2.
For finishing, follow the suggestions for the basic room divider.

Other crocheted cords

A double chain

This is also sometimes called a single crochet chain. Begin with a loop and crochet 2 stitches. Place the hook in the first stitch, pull the thread through this stitch and then through both the loops on the hook. See

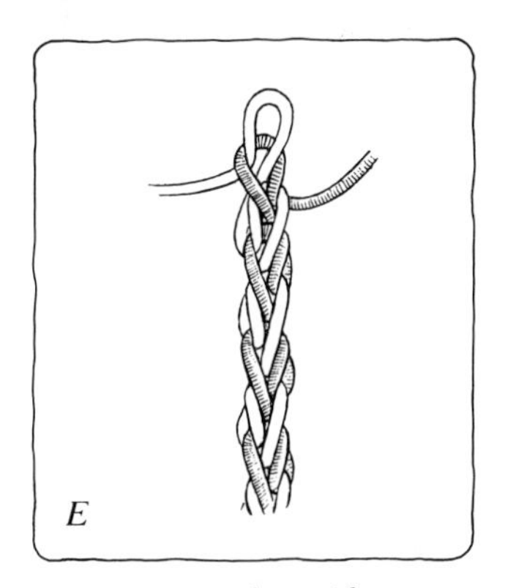

E. Finger crochet with 2 threads

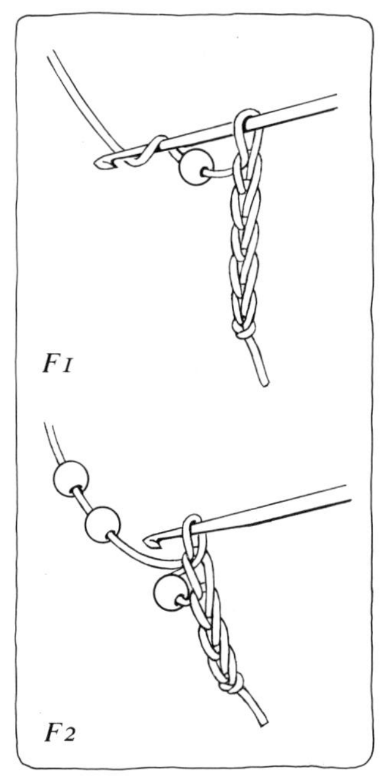

F1 and F2. Crocheting with beads

illustration F, number 1 and 2. Put the hook through the left stitch, pull the thread through this stitch and then pull the thread through both stitches; see illustration G, number 3. Continue in this manner for the desired length.

Double crochet chain

Begin a double crocheted chain with a starting row of 3 chain stitches. Loop the thread once around the hook, put the hook through one loop of the first chain and pick up this loop; there are now 3 stitches on the hook. See illustration G number 4. Bind off as in ordinary crochet, wrapping the yarn around the hook and pulling this through 2 stitches, wrapping the yarn around the hook and pulling it through the last 2 stitches. Wrap the yarn around the hook and put the hook into the left loop and pull this loop up; there are now 3 stitches on the hook again. Bind off the double crochet. This will give you a wide chain. Chains of half double crochet or triple crochet can also be made. See the stitch glossary for these stitches.

Chain with picots

A chain of loops can be made wider by adding picots as it is made. For information on this, see page 8 in the chapter on window decorations.

Using the room divider

There are many ways to use these room dividers. If, for instance, you have an open kitchen and the hall is fairly wide, you can separate part of this area with a room divider which, if necessary, can be pushed to one side. The cords can be crocheted as discussed earlier in this chapter. Use cotton or macramé thread so the curtain can be washed easily.

Such a curtain can also be made for a closet, such as a front hall closet, or to close off a niche in a hall or room. A cord curtain with beads is extremely decorative.

Working with colors

Naturally, your room divider does not need to be made in a basic color as in the photograph. You can make your cords in any colors that will suit your room.

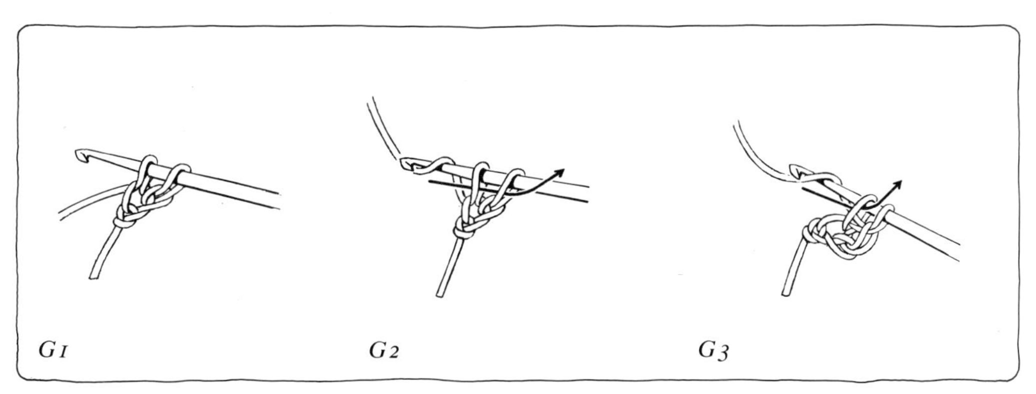

G1, 2, 3. A double starting chain

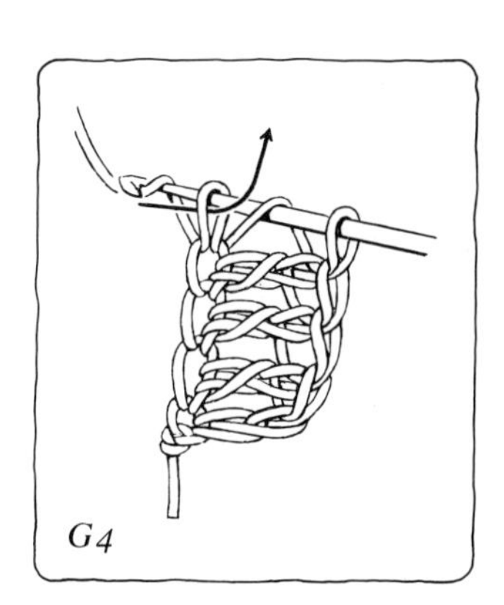

G4. Double crochet chain

6 The Bedroom

Who wouldn't find this nice to come home to?

Before you make a spread or cushions for your bedroom you must take into consideration the bed and the decoration of the bedroom itself.
In the past, the cushions and the spread were almost always made from white cotton. If you would like to reproduce the atmosphere of your grandmother's time, consider the picture on page 48. The blanket, of course, can be made large enough to use as a spread. The blanket and cushions are crocheted with heavy, unevenly spun, white wool. The crochet stitches used for the cushions are repeated in the blanket that lies on the rocking chair. The stitches used are popcorn, scallops, and cluster. See illustrations H 1, 2, 3 – I 1, 2, 3 – J 1, 2, 3, 4.

The scalloped cushion
Crochet a chain of 55 stitches so that the finished cushion will measure about 16 × 16 inches.
1st row: chain 3 (this is the 1st double crochet), crochet 2 double crochet in the 4th chain from the hook, * skip 2 stitches, work 1 single crochet in the following stitch, skip 2 stitches and crochet 5 double crochet (1 scallop) in the following stitch, repeat from * and end with 3 double crochet (a half scallop) in the last stitch. See illustration I numbers 1, 2, and 3.
2nd row: turn with 1 chain, crochet in the back loop of the stitches in the previous row, * work 1 scallop in the single crochet of the previous row, 1 single crochet in the middle of the following scallop, repeat from * and end with 1 single crochet in the last stitch of the half scallop.
3rd row: 3 chains (1st double crochet) and 2 double crochets in the single crochet, * 1 single crochet in the middle of the scallop, 1 scallop in the following single crochet, repeat from * and end with a half scallop. Repeat these 2nd and 3rd rows until 9 scallop rows are worked.

Continuing in popcorn stitch
1st row: continue to work in the back of the stitch. Crochet 3 chains for the 1st double crochet, crochet in each of the following 8 stitches 1 double crochet, * crochet in the following stitch 1 popcorn (this is: 4 double crochet in 1 stitch, pull the hook out of the last double crochet, put the hook through the top of the 1st double crochet and pick up again the last double crochet stitch. Pull the loop of the last stitch through, see illustration H 1, 2, 3) crochet on each of the following 11 stitches 1 double crochet, repeat from * and end with 9 double crochet.
2nd row: 3 chains (1st double crochet), crochet 7 double crochet * 1 popcorn, then crochet the popcorn to the other side by taking the hook from back to front through the first double crochet, 1 double crochet, 1 popcorn, 9 double crochet, repeat from * and end with 8 double crochet. Take care that the popcorn stitches lie on the right side of the work; the uneven rows should be worked in the usual way and on the even rows work the stitches from back to the front.
3rd row: 3 chains (1st double crochet), crochet 6 double crochet * 1 popcorn, 3 double crochet, 1 popcorn, 7 double crochet, repeat from *. Now put the hook in by the

H 1, 2, 3. Popcorn stitch, used on the cushion and blanket on page 48.

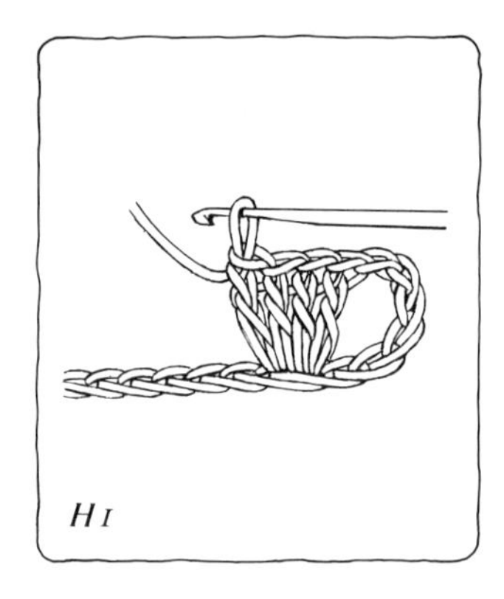

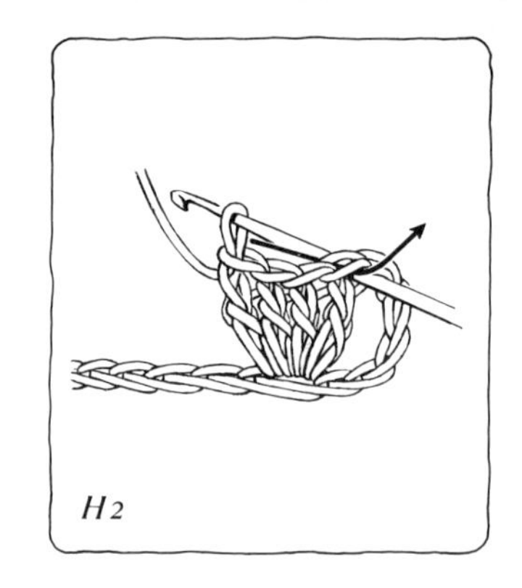

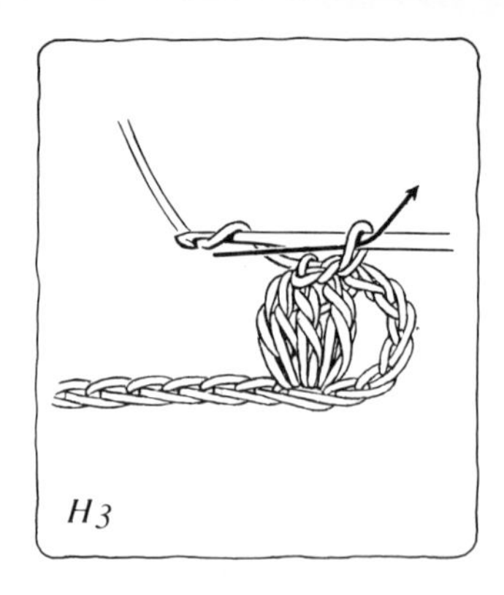

I 1, 2, 3. Crocheted scallops.

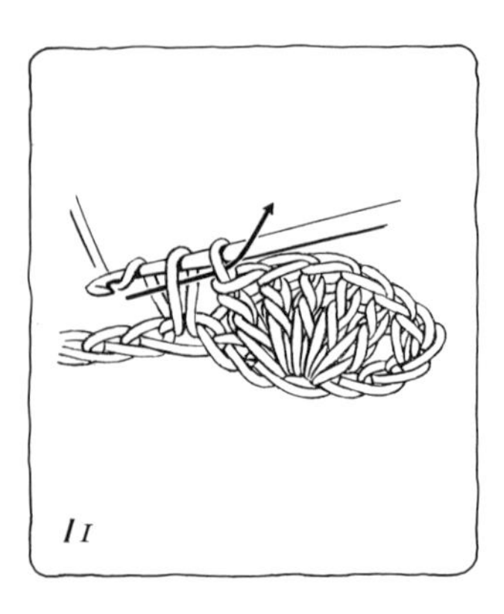

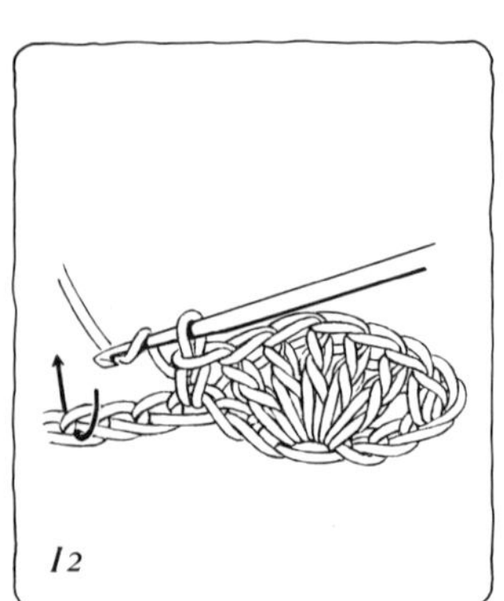

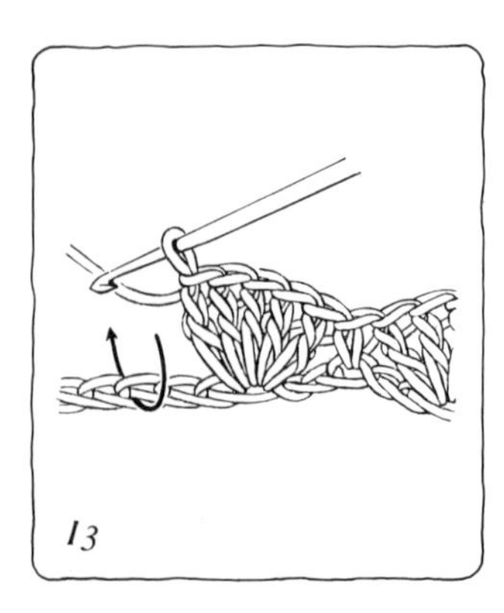

popcorn through the stitch of the first double crochet from back to front so that the popcorn stitch is placed on the right side.
4th row: 3 chains, * 5 double crochet, 1 popcorn, repeat from * and end with 6 double crochets.
5th row: 3 chains, 4 double crochet, * 1 popcorn, 7 double crochets, 1 popcorn, 3 double crochets, repeat from * and end with 5 double crochets.
6th row: 3 chains, 3 double crochet, * 1 popcorn, 9 double crochet, 1 popcorn, 1 double crochet, repeat from * and end with 4 double crochet. This is the middle row of the popcorn pattern. Crochet in reverse from here on, that is crochet the 5th, 4th, 3rd, 2nd, and 1st row in that order. Crochet until there are 9 rows of scallops. The single crochets of the 1st scallop row are on the popcorn stitches. Crochet the back of the cushion cover in the same way, or crochet this entirely in double crochet.

Cushion with popcorn in diamonds
Crochet a chain of 58 stitches for a cushion to measure 16 by 16 inches.
1st row: crochet double crochets, begin the 1st double crochet at the 5th chain from the hook. There are 55 double crochets in this row.
2nd row: crochet as the 1st double crochet 3 chains, 2 double crochet, 1 popcorn, for this see the popcorn stitch described in the scalloped cushion and illustrations 4 and 5, * 1 double crochet, 1 popcorn, repeat from * and end with 3 double crochet.
3rd row: as the 2nd row, crochet popcorn over popcorn and double crochet over double crochet. Take care in working the popcorn stitches that they stay on the right side of the work.
4th row: work the same as the 2nd row.
5th row: work the same as the 1st row; that is, work only double crochet.
6th row: as the 2nd row.
7th row: 3 chains, 2 double crochet, 4 times (1 popcorn, 1 double crochet), then 1 popcorn, 3 times (7 double crochet, 1 popcorn), 7 double crochet, 4 times (1 popcorn, 1 double crochet), ending with 1 popcorn, 3 double crochet.
8th through 10th row: as the 7th row, being sure the popcorn is on the right side of the work.
11th row: as the 3rd row.
12th through 15th row: as the 7th row.
16th through 21st row: as the 6th through the 1st row. Crochet the back the same way or work it completely in double crochet.

This is about 24 rows of double crochet.

Cushion with clusters and diamonds
Crochet a chain of 64 stitches.
1st row: begin in the 5th stitch from the hook and crochet double crochets.
2nd row: crochet 3 chains as the 1st double crochet, * 1 double crochet, crochet in the following stitch a cluster as follows: wrap the yarn around the hook, put the hook in the stitch, wrap the yarn around the hook and pull it through the stitch, wrap the yarn around the hook and bind off 2 stitches, wrap the yarn around the hook, put the hook in the same stitch, wrap the yarn around the hook and crochet through this

Crocheting double loops.

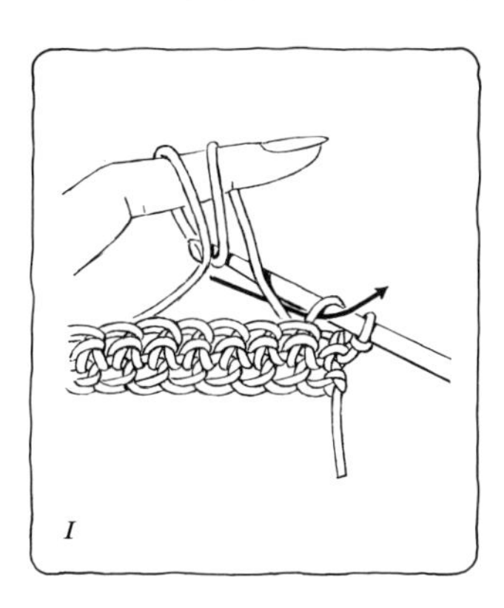

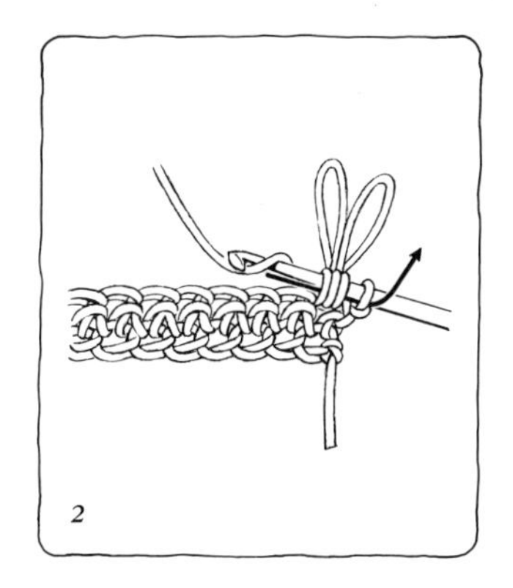

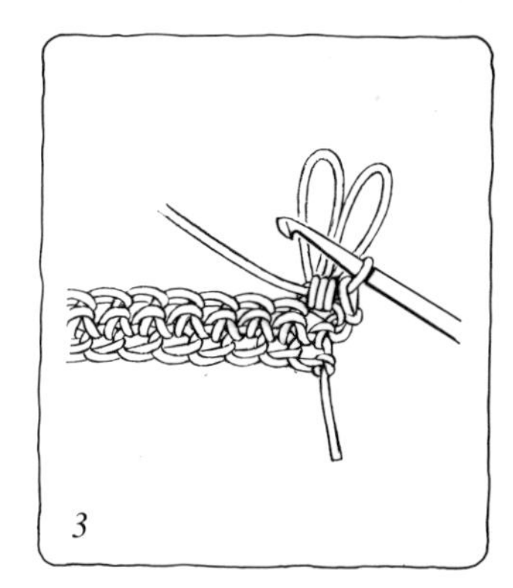

stitch, wrap the yarn around the hook and bind off 2 stitches, wrap the yarn around and bind off all the stitches, 1 double crochet, repeat from *. See illustration J 1, 2, 3, 4.
3rd row: work in double crochet.
4th row: work alternating 2 double crochet and 1 cluster.
5th row: work in double crochet.
Repeat again from the 2nd row until 10 rows are worked. Next, crochet 10 rows in double crochet and, finally, repeat the first 10 rows. Crochet the back in double crochet, making about 28 rows.

Diamonds
On the bottom of the work start your crochet by taking a stitch with the crochet hook. Pull the thread up as a loop. Put the hook a little further into the crochet work, pull a loop up, and bring this through the loop on the needle. This makes chain stitches on the top of your crochet work. Crochet these chains over the middle section of double crochets, working back and forth in such a way that a diamond is made.

Finishing the edges
Crochet a *double loop border* around the edges; see pictures 1, 2 and 3. First, work 1 row of single crochet around the top of the cushion cover; at the corners, crochet 3 single crochet in 1 stitch. Next, crochet the loop row on the back of the work. Put the hook into the top loop, wrap the yarn 2 times around the pointer of your left hand or wrap it around the pointer and middle finger at the same time. Wrap the thread from back to front. Hold the loops up as shown in illustration 1 and pull these through the stitch; there are 3 loops. Wrap the yarn around the hook and pull it through the 4 loops on the hook; see picture 2. Continue in this way, working a double loop in every single crochet.

Blankets
Following the instructions for the cushions you can develop a pattern for crocheting a matching blanket or spread. Use a double yarn and a large crochet hook. Crochet a chain of 109 stitches and begin and end the

Illustration J 1, 2, 3, 4. The working of cluster stitches.

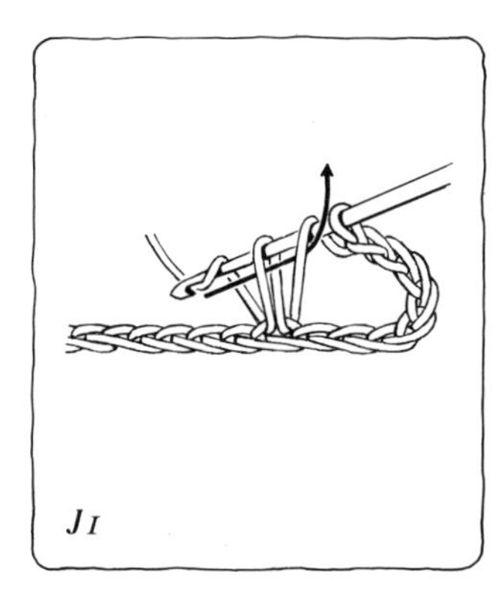

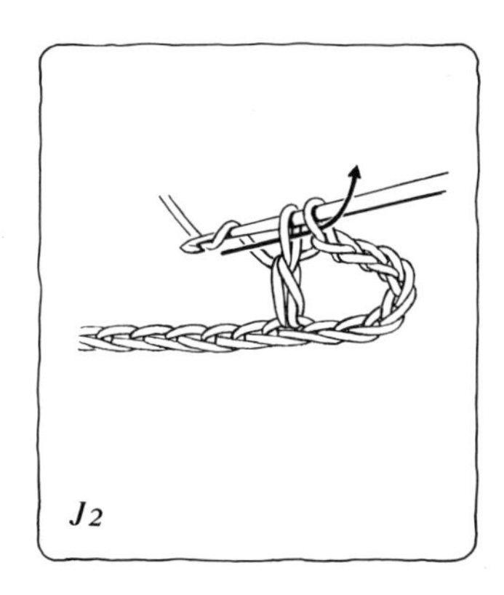

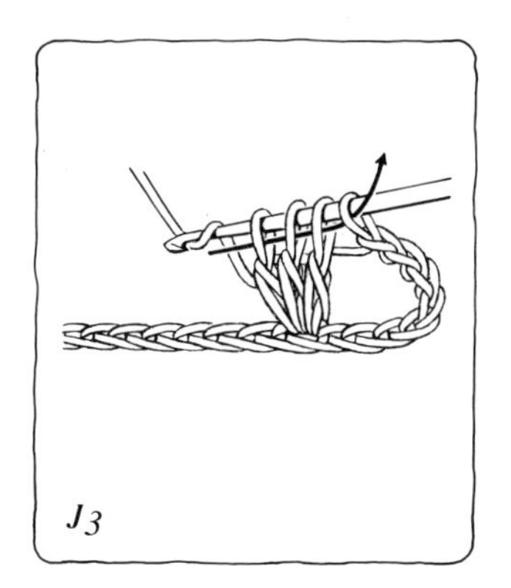

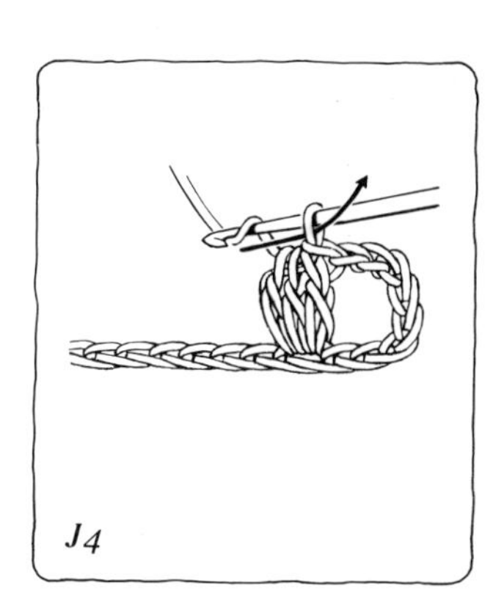

first row with a half scallop. The width of the work will be about 34 inches. There are 17 scallops with a half scallop at each side. After you have crocheted 7 rows of scallops, crochet 8 rows of double crochet, 8 rows of popcorn stitch with 7 double crochet between every popcorn, 8 rows of double crochet and 8 rows of popcorn. Half the blanket is now finished; crochet the other half reversing the order of the rows. This is only an example of how you can use the patterns given for the cushions to make a blanket or spread. There are many other variations possible with these patterns, including, of course, variations of color.
To finish the blanket, you can either work a loop border as was done in the case of the cushions, or make a row of single crochet with picot.

Patchwork spread

When this type of spread is made of fabric it is called a patchwork quilt. Crocheting a spread in a patchwork design has advantages, one of which is that, since it is crocheted in sections, you don't have a heavy work hanging on your crochet hook. The patches are forms which have been crocheted to more or less fit together so that, when they are joined, they form a spread. A patchwork spread suits almost every interior, traditional or modern. The mood of it is determined by the colors and designs in the spread. For a child's room, a spread made from simple squares in vivid colors would be ideal. Crocheted hexagons can be made into flower designs by sewing six hexagons around one central hexagon. Seven hexagons form one flower. These can be joined together to make a large spread.
The shape of the spread shown in the picture is taken from a mosaic in the Alhambra. The shape is that of a stylized dumbbell. The top and bottom sections fit exactly into the middle sections.
The shapes are worked entirely in single crochet.

Dumbbell design

Crochet a chain of 16 stitches, turn with 1 chain, and crochet in single crochet. In-

A patchwork cover worked in a dumbbell design with a wonderful doll. Both, of course, are crocheted (see also page 58).

Copy this pattern to the size you want. First draw the squares, then fill in the squares with the dumbbell design. Crochet the designs according to the instructions on the previous page or follow the pattern. The drawing shows how the designs fit together.

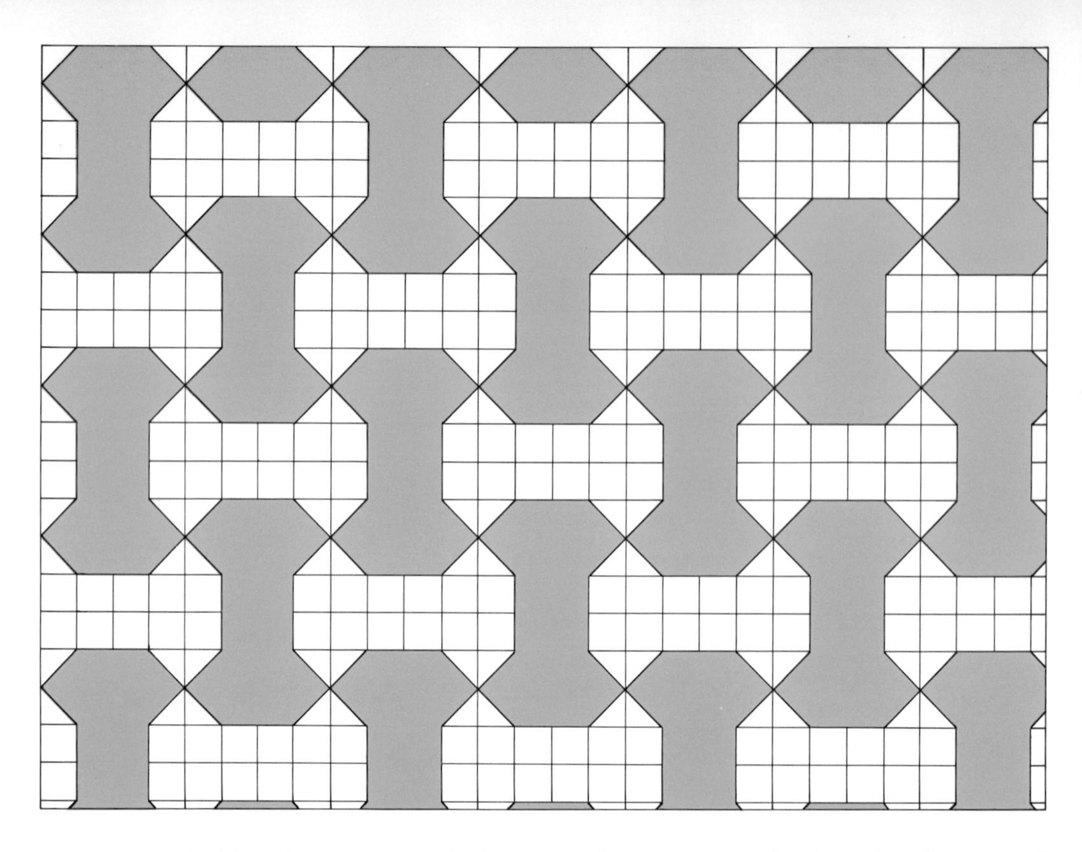

crease on both sides of every row 1 single crochet until there are 32 single crochets. Decrease until there are 16 single crochet. Do not end, but instead crochet 1 row of single crochet around increasing by 1 or 2 stitches at the outside corners and decreasing at the inside corners by 1 or 2 stitches.

Color combinations

The picture gives you an example of possible colors, but naturally you are not limited to these. More or fewer colors can be used in your version of this spread.

Light and dark colors always combine well together. Make the background color light so that the other shapes will stand out against it. The design, which has been crocheted in reddish brown, blue, and dark gray in the picture, can also be crocheted in one color, but then, of course, you have a less dramatic total effect. Colors that are related to each other, such as shades of blue and green, can be very effective. Be sure the spread works with the other elements in the bedroom, such as the draperies, the rug, and the upholstery of any furniture.

Your own design

It is a great deal of fun to design your own pattern for such a spread. You can do the drawing to scale. Fill in the areas with the colors you plan for your yarn, using felt tipped pens or colored pencils.
Begin by drawing a large rectangle and drawing lines in it. These can be triangles with rectangles or squares or more complicated shapes, provided the shapes can be crocheted and work well in the total design.

Color contrast

Your color choice is very important. In a somewhat somber room, warm colors can be introduced and will look well. These include shades of red such as tomato red and the like that can be used with green. For the background choose light beige.
If the room doesn't need color or if it has a dominant color on the walls of floor, then choose either lighter or darker shades of the

colors. You know the rules: light colors enlarge, dark colors reduce. Gold is very attractive combined with a light version of itself and moss and olive green; think of the autumn colorings of the trees.
In fact, colors in nature can often help you make a good color choice. Look not only at leaves, but also at flowers and butterflies. All these things can inspire you and give you ideas for beautiful color combinations.

Loop crochet wall hanging
This wall hanging, like the spread, is made up of small crocheted sections. This time they are parallelograms. In order to get a good shape for this you must draw a circle with a compass on which the radius, or the distance between the point of the compass and the point of the pencil, is as large as the widest part of the parallelogram that you will make. Mark off the radius 6 times to the edge of the circle; see the illustration. The radius is A-M. M is the middle point. The other outside points are B, C, D, E, F. By connecting A-B, B-C, C-D, D-E, E-F, and F-A with each other you will create a hexagon, join point M with point B, point F, and point D. There are now 3 parallelograms in the hexagon. With these forms you can make many things for patchwork. The wall hanging is one example, but there are many other ways to color and place these shapes.

Playing with color
Such a wall hanging offers many possibilities for playing with color. Try out various colors with the help of colored pencils, crayons, or felt tip pens, before you buy your yarn. Consider red with the color next to it violet. Choose shades between these colors and for contrast pick a shade of yellow as yellow contrasts with violet. You can add a blue-purple to the wall hanging. These colors would work well together. If you'd rather have your wall hanging in a blue or green shade, then the colors in the picture are satisfactory. This design can be very beautiful worked in yellow, orange-yellow, orange-red, and red yarns, or in tints

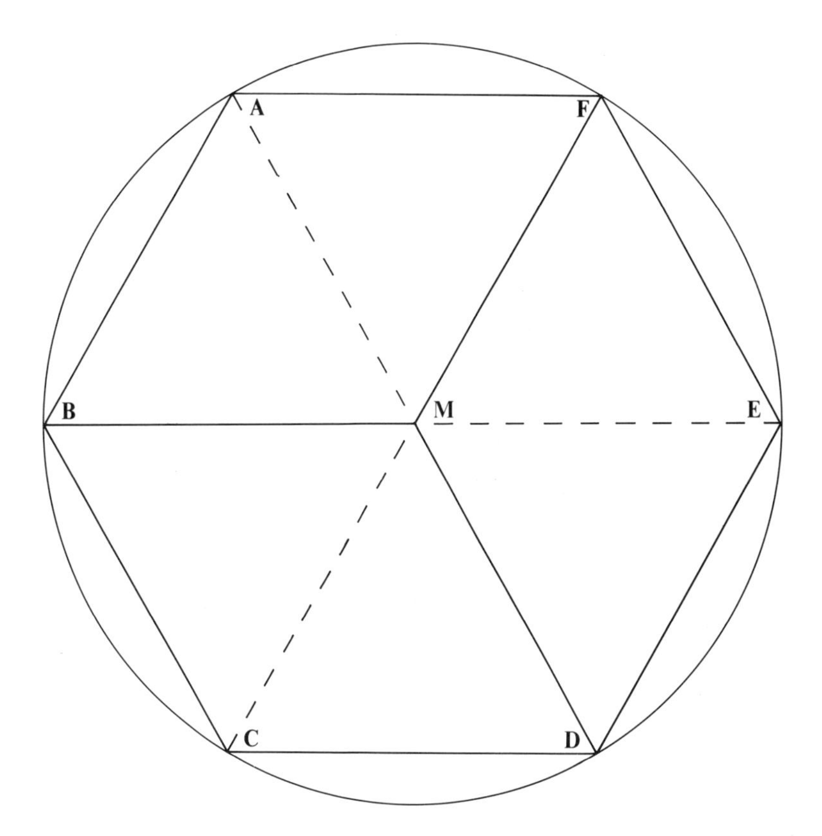

An example of the construction of a hexagon with 3 parallelograms inside the hexagon.

Still another example of patchwork, this time worked in crocheted loops. The wall hanging can, as can be seen from the pattern on page 58, also be hung horizontally.

of dark red to light rose. Combinations of the colors black, gray, white, brown, and orange-red in a modern bedroom with white or off-white furniture can be very dramatic.

Crocheting loops

This stitch produces a loopy fleece. The loops can be cut open after they are crocheted.

Every loop row consists of 1 row of single crochet on the right side. On the reverse side the loops are crocheted which are brought around to lie on the right side of the work.

Begin with a chain.

Crochet 1 row of single crochet. Turn with 1 chain. Put the yarn over your left pointer, or around a strip of cardboard. If you use the cardboard, the width of it will determine the size of the loop. The advantage to using a piece of cardboard, or a ruler, is that all the loops will be the same length. This is difficult to ensure if you make the loops on your finger.

The yarn is wrapped in the opposite direction; see page 59, illustration 1. By opposite direction we mean from back to front. Put the crochet hook in the first stitch of the previous single crochet row. Hold your finger high and pull both yarns under your finger or under the piece of cardboard and through the stitch; see illustration 1. There are now 3 loops on the needle; see illustration 2. Wrap the yarn around the hook as in ordinary crochet and pull it through the 3 loops; see illustration 3. Repeat in every following single crochet. Turn at the end of the row with 1 chain and crochet 1 row of single crochet on the right side. Repeat these rows.

Crocheting diamonds

Make a chain of 2 stitches. Turn and crochet 3 single crochet in the 1st stitch from the hook. Turn and crochet loops back. In the following single crochet rows increase 1 stitch on both ends by crocheting 2 single crochet in the first and last single crochet. Increase until there are 17 single crochet and end with a row of loops. Now begin to decrease in each single crochet row by skipping the first and last stitches on each side. Decrease until there are 3 stitches remaining. End with a row of 3 loops and bind off the 3 stitches.

Half diamonds, triangles, and quarter diamonds

For a *half diamond* increase and decrease on only one side so that the other side remains straight.

For a *triangle* crochet as for a diamond but end with a row of slip stitches after the last increase, that is when there are 17 loops.

If you are making a *two colored half diamond*, then begin the second color when you have 17 loops.

For a *quarter diamond*, crochet as for a half diamond but end with a row of slip stitches after you have finished increasing.

Pillow cover

By placing 6 diamonds in a star design and filling in the sides of the diamonds you can create a circle. In making the *diamonds for the sides* increase and decrease on one side as for the complete diamond but follow these instructions on the opposite side for decreasing and increasing. After 3 loop rows increase 4 times by 1 stitch and, after the middle of the diamond on the same side, decrease by 1 stitch in every 3rd loop row 4 times. Sew the sections to each other and crochet a row of single crochet around the edges.

If you plan to use the cover for a chair or stool make a hem in the last rows and run an elastic through it so that the cover can be stretched over the seat. Choose colors that coordinate with the wall hanging.

Other possibilities

If you crochet the diamonds with a thick yarn and cut the loops after they are crocheted, you can make a rug.

If you crochet the diamonds without loops they can be made into a spread. In this case, the diamonds can be made larger by increasing more times and then, of course, decreasing in the same way.

If you don't want to use single crochet but, for example, double crochet or half double crochet, then follow a paper model. Make this by first drawing a hexagon. This type of crocheted patchwork can also be used for cushion covers or for a cover for a hassock. The construction is similar to that of the stool or chair covering and the loops are replaced by ordinary single crochet. Make a border on the edge by crocheting in single crochet and work the bottom in an ordinary way. Begin in the middle with a chain and crochet single crochet around. You will undoubtedly be able to work out other possibilities yourself.

The doll

The doll on the bed on pages 52 is entirely crocheted.

Begin with the body. Crochet a chain as long as twice the width of the top, that is, the shoulder. Make this into a circle and crochet in single crochet. After a couple of inches decrease some stitches to form a waist. After the waist, increase for the hips and at the desired length cast off. Sew up both shoulder seams, leaving a section open in the middle for the neck. Crochet the

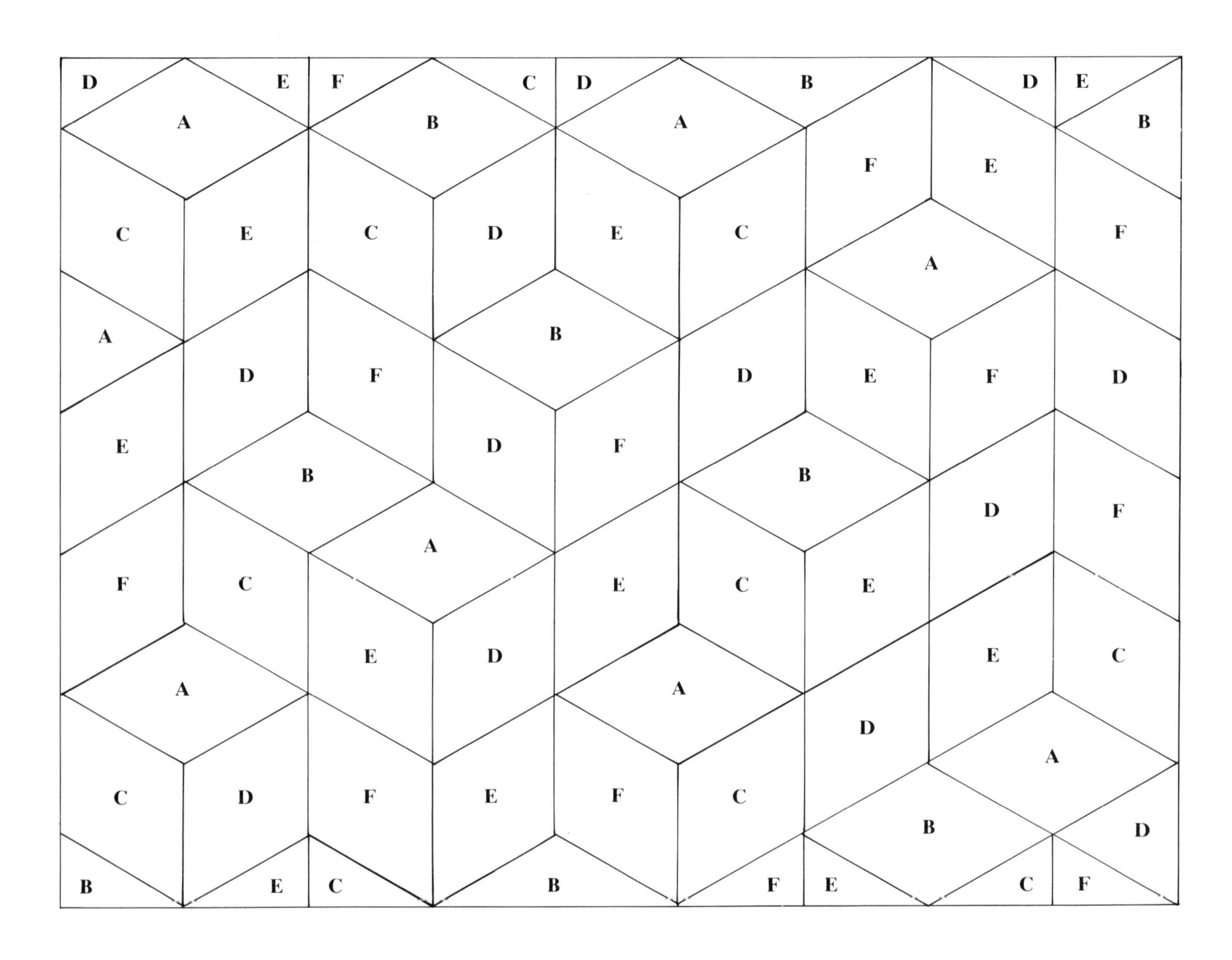

This is the pattern for the wall hanging. The letters indicate the different colors.

Crocheting loops, such as for the cushion cover on page 56.

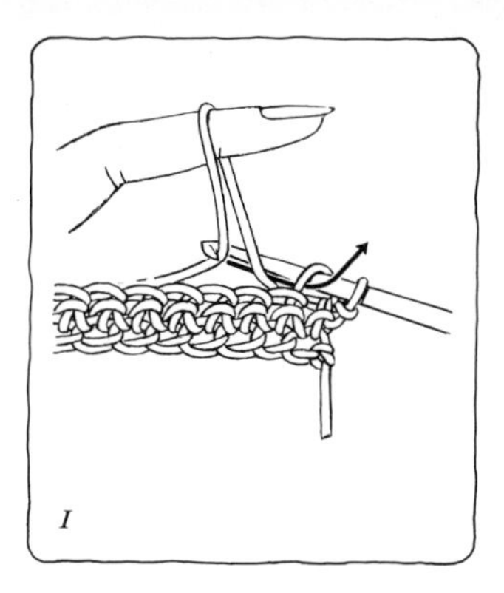

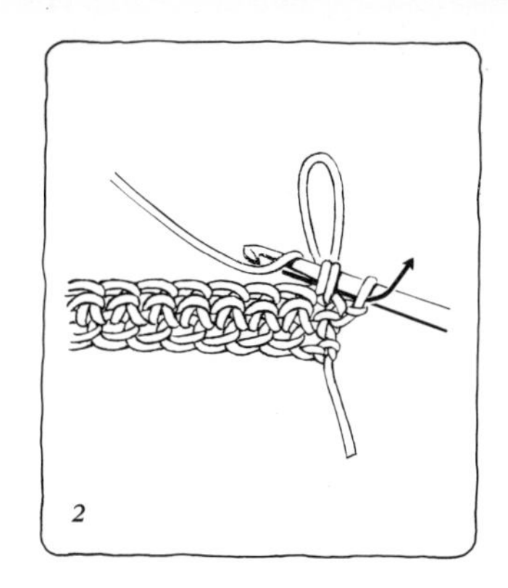

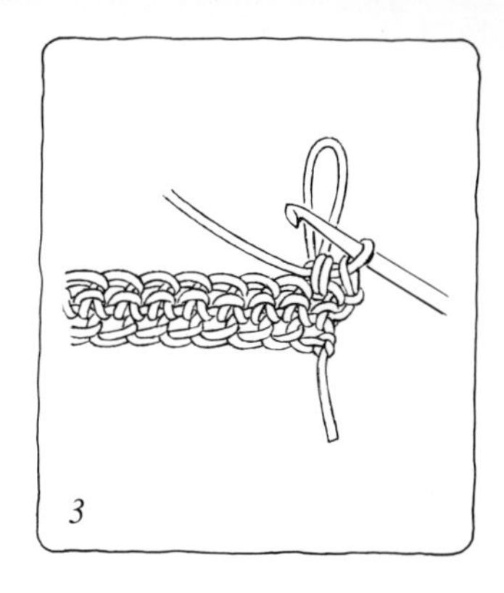

neck in the round in this opening for about 1¼ inches and finish off. Crochet arms and legs; shape these as for the body, making the top part of the leg thicker than the bottom. You can also shape a calf and a knee by decreasing and increasing. Give the hands fingers by crocheting at the bottom of the arms 5 chains of a couple of stitches and crocheting single crochet along these chains. Stuff the body, arms, and legs firmly and sew the arms and legs to the body. For the head, crochet 2 circles with a strip in between about ¾ inch wide. Sew the parts to each other, stuff firmly, and sew the head to the neck. You may want to first put a rolled up piece of cardboard into the neck. Crochet a little nose, eyes, and mouth and sew these to the face. Now the doll must be dressed. This is entirely up to your own imagination. The doll shown is wearing pantaloons with a border of scallops along the bottom edges. On top of this there is a crocheted dress with a wide skirt and wide sleeves of double crochet and chain with, along the edges, scallops. Crochet loops for the hair on the head and then make a hat from heavy yarns. Boots, with or without a heel, or shoes can also be crocheted and sewn securely to the legs. This is only an example. Old fashioned dolls, such as those you can find in antique shops or see in museums, can be a real source of inspiration. If you find this doll a little too difficult you can, of course, crochet a simple, long body. Make a length of single crochet for the body measuring, say, 6 by 8 inches. Fold this piece of fabric in half and stitch the side seam closed. Crochet long strips about 3 inches wide for the arms and legs and sew them up along the long edges. Crochet 2 circles for the head. Stuff the various parts and sew them to the body. By using variously colored yarns for this you can crochet the clothes in to the doll as you work by, for example, putting stripes on the body for a sweater. Carry the stripes a little over the arms for sleeves. Crochet the top of the legs in a solid color for pants and the bottom in another solid color for shoes.

7 Hairpin Lace

Hairpin lace is a type of crochet which is worked on a special hairpin lace fork. This fork is U shaped and has a movable bar to hold both legs of the fork at the right distance. The forks used for hairpin lace today have adjustable legs. The old fashioned forks were only available in individual sizes.
Hairpin lace is certainly not difficult; it is simply a question of making even stitches. Once the hairpin lace is worked, the strips can be joined together to form such things as crocheted curtains, stoles, and, as shown in the picture, lamp shades.

What is hairpin lace?
Make a starting chain as in the case of ordinary crochet. Put the chain on one prong of the fork, keeping the knot exactly in the middle of the two prongs. While crocheting, hold the fork in your left hand with the beginning chain between thumb and pointer. Take the thread with the crochet hook and draw it through the starting chain, see illustration 1. Turn the fork from right to left, thereby wrapping the thread around the 2nd prong, and work a single crochet on the front thread of the chain. (See page 63, illustration 2.) Turn the fork from right to left after each single crochet and crochet 1 single crochet on the front thread of the chain; see illustration 3. In illustrations 4, 5 and 6 the single crochets are not made on the front of the loop but on both threads of the loop; this makes a heavier crocheted border in the center. Practice working with your hairpin lace fork and you will see how easy it is.

Different possibilities
The width of the lace depends on the width of the fork. The distance between the loops depends upon the stitches making the loops. Tight loops result if 1 single crochet is worked on 2 stitches. The loops are more widely separated if 2 single crochet are worked in every stitch. The distance between the loops is still larger if half double crochets or double crochets are worked.

Narrow heavy strips
Place the prongs close together and use a medium weight yarn. Join the loops with slip stitches. You now have a narrow edging that, for example, can be sewn around a cushion as a finishing border.

Wide strips
If the prongs of the fork are widely separated large loops on both sides will result. These can be joined in various ways, such as with 1, 2, or 3 single crochet, a half double crochet, or a double crochet.
Long loops, widely spaced, give you an airy result that can be quite effective for curtains.

Long strips
When the fork is completely filled with loops on both prongs the loops can be slid from the fork carefully and rolled around a piece of cardboard; keep the last 7 or 8 loops on the fork.
If you need to count the loops as, for instance, when you are making strips to be sewn together, attach the loops of one side onto a thread in groups of 20, 40, or more.

Hairpin lace is a different form of crochet. The lamps are covered with strips of hairpin lace made in various techniques and colors.

Crocheting the loops together
The simplest way to crochet the loops together is without the use of yarn; see illustration 7. Place the two strips next to each other, put the crochet hook into the loop of the left strip and take this over the hook. Put the hook in the first loop of the right strip and draw the loop of the left strip through this. Take the next loop of the left strip and draw this through the loop of the right strip. Continue in this way, alternating left and right strips.

A variation on this method is to take 2 or more loops of a strip rather than 1 and to pull these through the same number of loops on the other strip. This results in a somewhat rougher, bulkier interweaving than with the use of single loops.

Joining with slip stitches
Make a starting chain on the crochet hook. Put the hook through the first loop of the left strip and pull the thread through both loops on the needle, put the needle in the first loop of the right hand strip and pull the thread through both loops. Put the hook in the following loop of the left strip and pull the thread through and so forth, joining alternately 1 loop of the right strip and 1 loop of the left. See illustration 8. There are many other ways of joining the strips. Additional loops can be picked up for joining at the same time.

Embroider around the strips
Before the strips can be joined together with crochet they must have slip stitches worked around them. Make a chain on the crochet hook. Put the hook in the first loop and pull the thread through both loops, put the hook in the following loop and pull the thread through both loops. In this way single crochet can be crocheted on the loops in place of slip stitches or half double crochets. When the strips have been crocheted around on both sides these can be joined to each other with crochet. To do this, place both strips together with the edges of crochet touching. Make a starting chain on your crochet hook and put the hook through both the first stitches, work a slip stitch, put the hook through both following stitches and work a single crochet. This method of joining strips is less elastic than the join formed when the strips are joined directly with crochet.

The edge of the outside strip
Crochet a row of slip stitches on every loop or, if the strips are joined by the loops, use the same number of loops used in the joining. On this slip stitch row crochet, for instance, a row of scallops or picots.

Turned loops
In joining the strips together the loops can be turned. If you do this, the loops then form a pattern between the middle of the strip and the area where they are joined. This can also be done, of course, in joining 2 or more loops together.

An arched effect
Make a starting loop on the needle and crochet in the first 3 loops of the left strip 5 single crochet, pick up the turned loop, crochet 2 chains. Crochet in the first 3 loops of the right strip 5 single crochet, crochet 2 chains, and crochet in the following 3 loops of the left strip 5 single crochet, and so forth. To finish the border of the outside edge in this case, rather than working the 5 single crochet through 3 loops, work as the 2nd single crochet a picot and then 2 single crochet. With this example and your own imagination you will discover many different possibilities in working with hairpin lace.

Different colors
By working with varying colors you can make splendid looking objects, as the lamps show. Be sure that every strip has the same number of loops as otherwise the strips cannot be crocheted together.

Strips into circles
To make a circle baste a thread on one side of a strip of loops and finish the outside edge with slip stitches with, between every slip stitch, 1 or more loops. More strips

can be added to this circle. This can be made easier if more loops are finished off on one side and on the other side 1 is finished with or without loops between the single crochets. In this way, strips can be made into a cover for a round cushion.
A hairpin lace strip with a beautifully finished edge can be sewn to a linen table cloth, and creative crocheters will discover that not only rectangular but also round lamp shades can be covered with strips of hairpin lace.
Once you have mastered hairpin lace you will become enthusiastic about it and its many possibilities.

Hairpin lace (illustrations 1, 2, 3, 4, 5, 6). Illustrations 7 and 8 show how the strips are crocheted to each other.

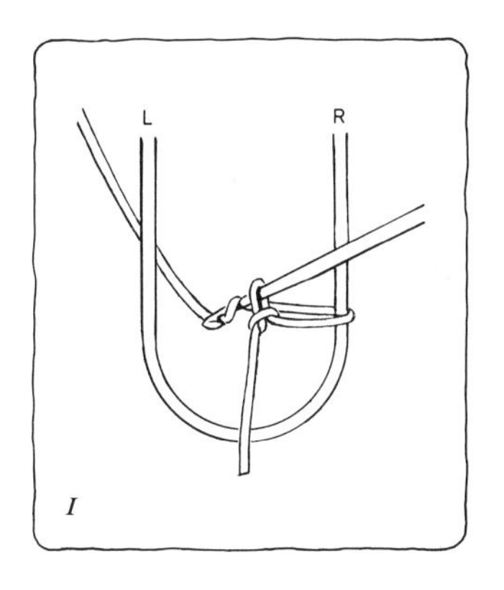

1

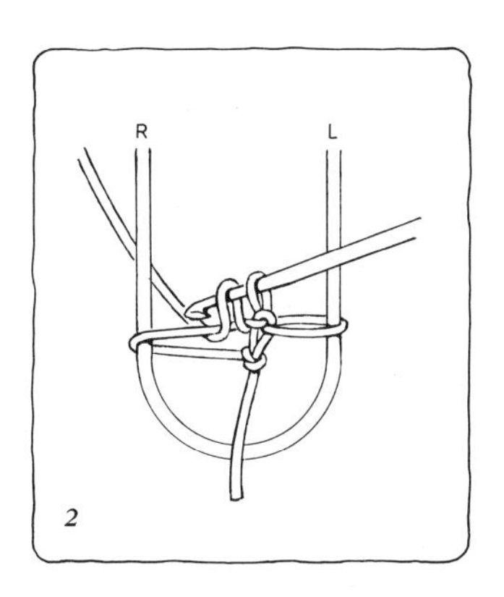

2

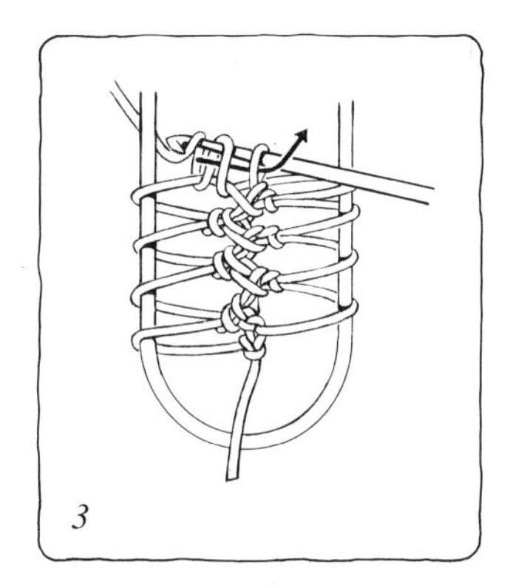
3

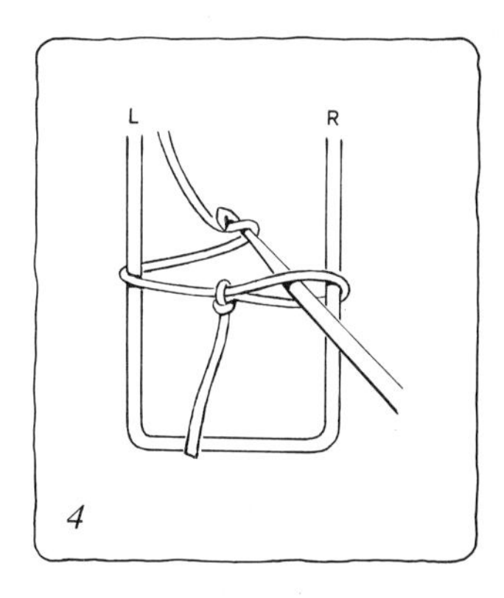

4

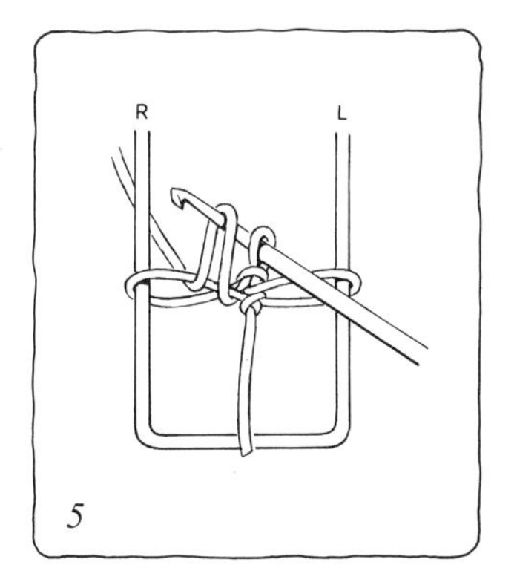

5

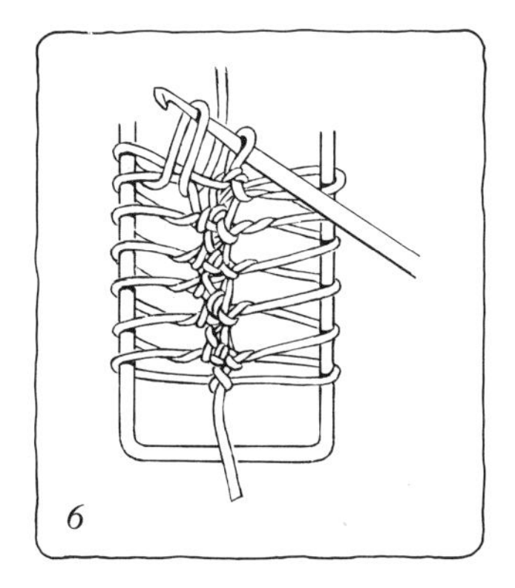
6

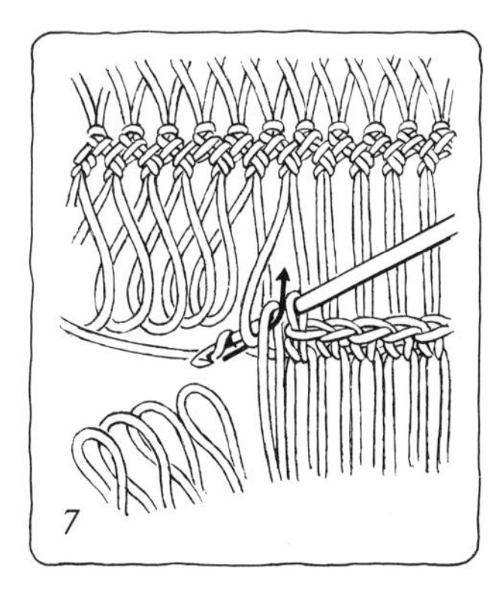
7

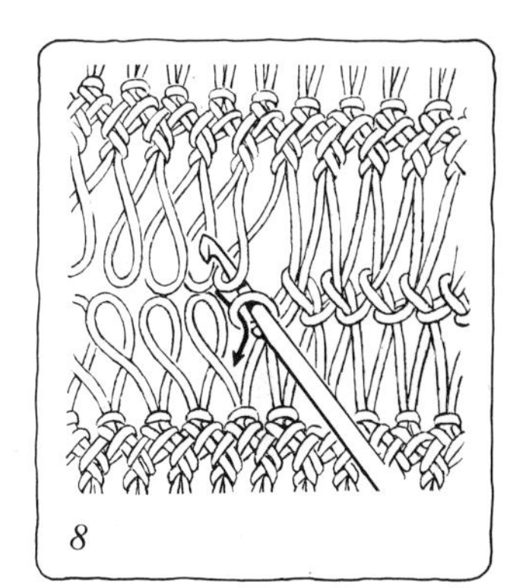
8

8 The Children's Room

The mascot
The starting point for the children's room is the circle, a form that children get to know in nursery school when they work with blocks. A crocheted mascot, that can be hung on the wall, forms the basis for the further designs for the children's room that you will find on the following pages. The doll is about 10¼ inches high. To make this mascot you'll need about 1 ball of white and 1 ball of green medium weight yarn, and small amounts of yellow, orange, cerise, blue, brown, dark beige, and red. You'll also need a medium sized crochet hook.
Crochet all sections with a double thread. Begin by making the circle for the body. Using green, make a chain of 4 stitches and close this into a ring with a slip stitch. Begin every following row with 1 chain and close every row with a slip stitch in the first chain.
Row 1: crochet 10 single crochet in the ring.
Row 2: crochet in every single crochet 2 single crochet, making 20 single crochet.
Row 3: crochet 30 single crochets by working 2 single crochets in every 2nd single crochet.
Row 4: crochet 30 single crochet.
Row 5: crochet 40 single crochet by cro-cheting 2 single crochet in every 3rd single crochet.
Row 6: crochet without increasing on 40 single crochet.
Continue to crochet in this way increasing by 10 stitches in every odd row. Crochet until the diameter of the circle is 5½ inches. Close the last row with a slip stitch with the blue yarn and finish off the green. Continue to crochet in blue, changing the crochet hook for a finer one. * 1 single crochet in the following single crochet, 3 chains, and 1 slip stitch in the 3rd chain (this is a picot), repeat from * and close the row with a slip stitch in the first stitch. Finish off. Blue chain stitches, worked on the body, form the arms.
For these, hold the thread in back of the crocheted body, put the crochet hook from the front to the back of the crochet work. Begin at the outside edge of the bottom of the arm. Crochet the yarn through to the top, forming a loop on the needle. Put the hook in 1 stitch further along, again from top to bottom, draw the yarn to the top and pull the loop through the stitch on the hook. Put the hook in again one stitch further along and in this way crochet a row of chain stitches. For the shape of the arms see the picture.

Flower buttons
Crochet in cerise, using a single thread of yarn, a chain of 5 stitches and close this with a slip stitch into a ring. Crochet 10 single crochet in the ring. Close every row with a slip stitch and begin every row with 1 chain if the row will be single crochet and 3 chains if the row will be double crochet. If the row is double crochet close it at the third stitch from the beginning.
Crochet 4 double crochet in 1 single crochet, crochet a slip stitch at the back of the first double crochet of this group so that the double crochet are drawn together, chain 1, * work 5 double crochet in the following single crochet with a half double crochet in the back of the first double crochet, chain 1, repeat from * in all single crochets of

A mascot for the wall. On the following pages are a variety of things which can be made with this as the starting point.

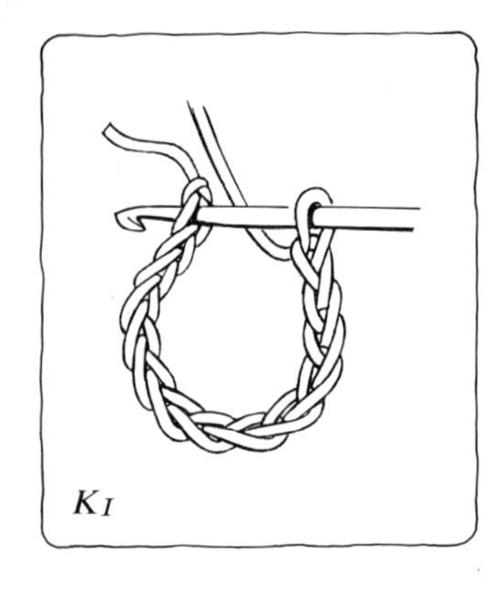

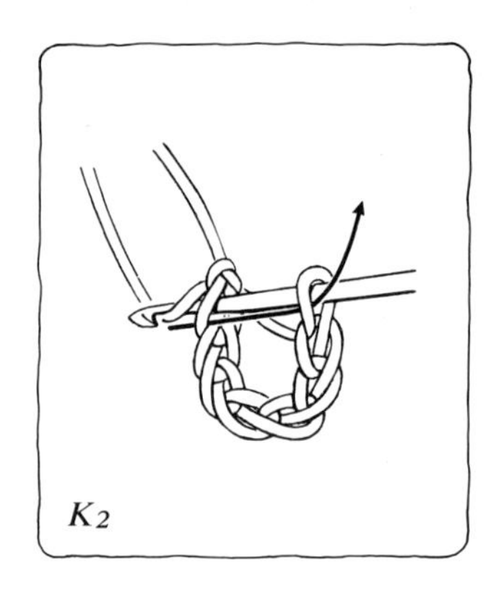

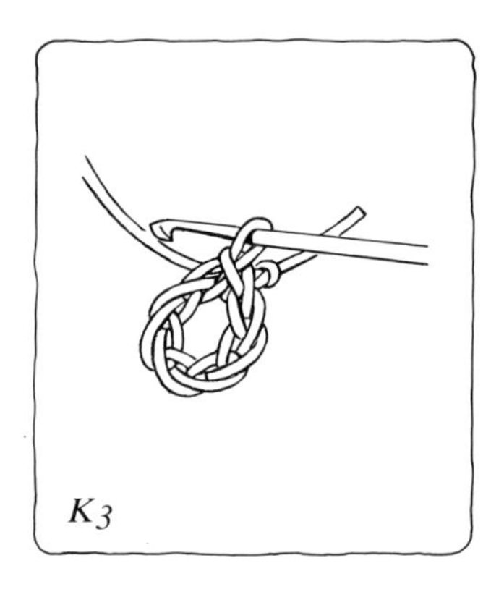

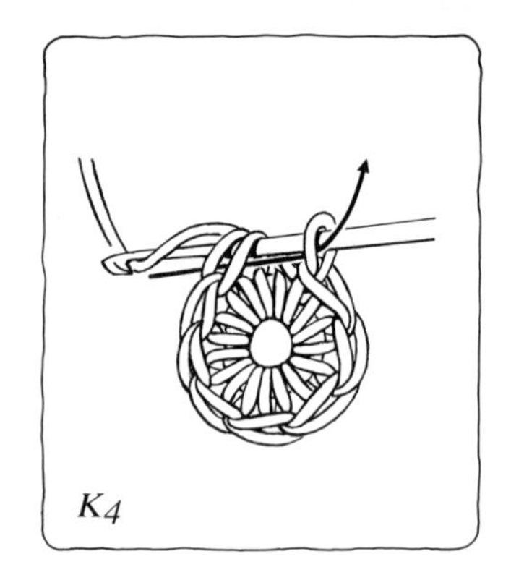

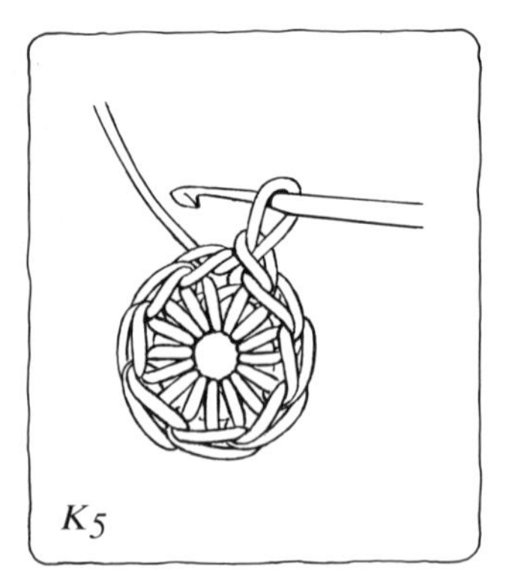

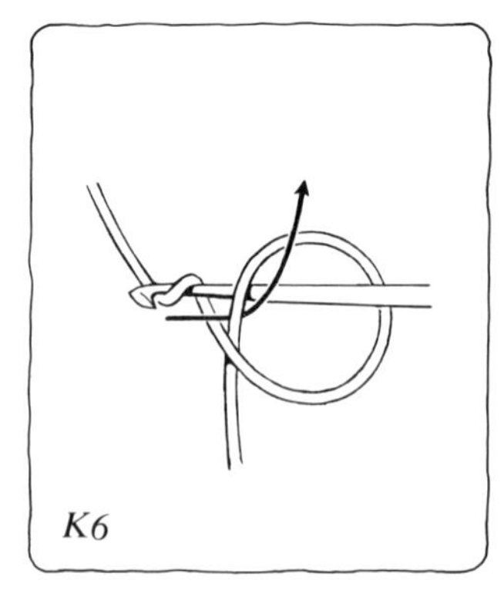

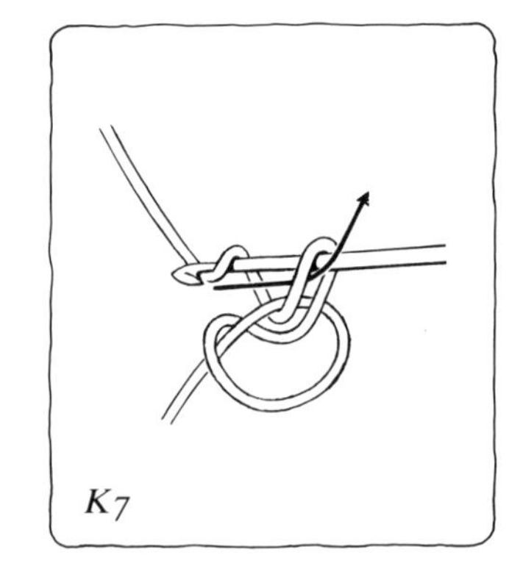

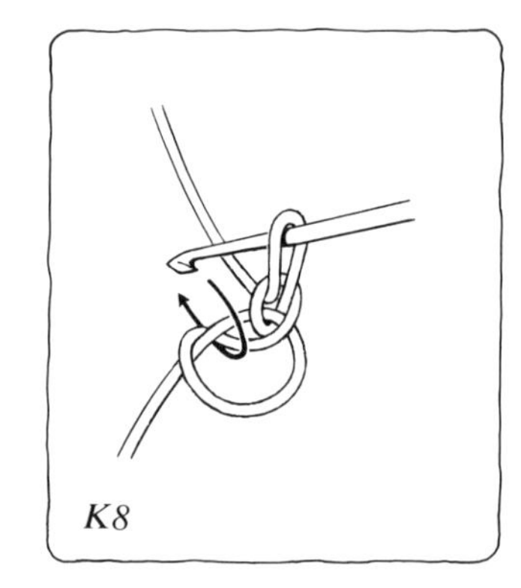

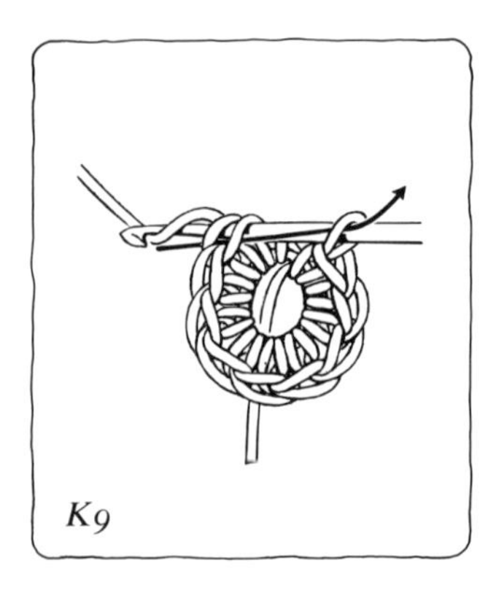

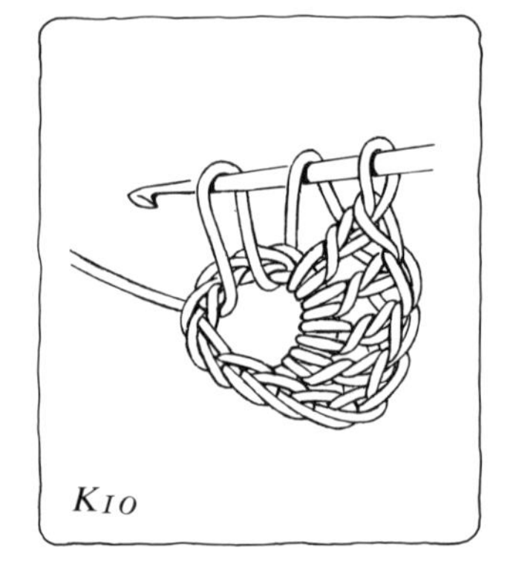

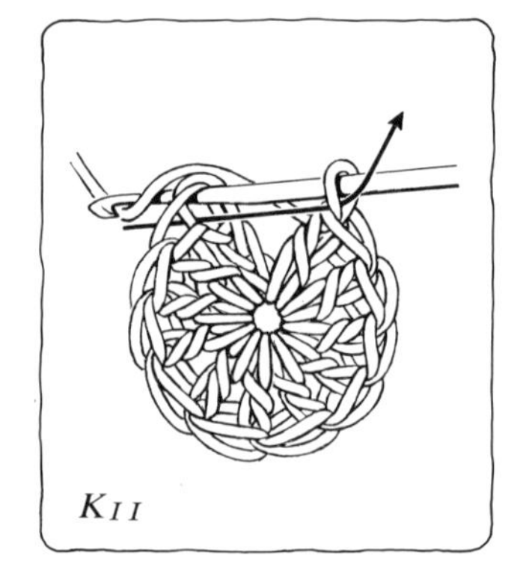

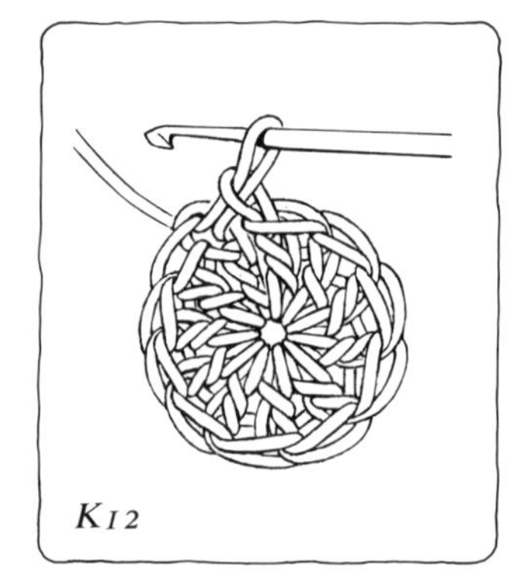

The technique of crocheting circles.

the previous row. Close the row and finish. Crochet a second flower in the same way.

Head

Make a chain of 5 stitches with one white thread of yarn and one beige. Close the chain into a ring with a slip stitch. Crochet in single crochet, as for the body, until the diameter is $4\frac{1}{4}$ inches. Form *the ears* as follows: crochet 13 single crochet, turn, crochet 1 chain, crochet 2 single crochet in the following single crochet and crochet 1 single crochet in each of the following 11 single crochet stitches. Then work 2 single crochet in the following single crochet and turn. Crochet 1 chain, work 2 single crochet in the following single crochet and in each of the following 13 single crochet work 1 single crochet. Work 2 single crochet in the next single crochet and finish. At the same height on the other side of the circle make a second ear in the same way.

After that, crochet 1 row of single crochet around the head with a single strand of

brown yarn. Do not crochet along the top where the hair will be. Begin above the ear and end at the other side at the same level. Embroider the face with chain and satin stitches, following the picture. Use yellow yarn to make the hair.
Sew the head to the body.

Feet

Crochet a circle with a single strand of orange yarn as you did for the body until it has a diameter of ½ inch. Crochet around it a row of picots as follows: * 1 single crochet, 1 picot of 3 chains with 1 slip stitch in the 3rd chain, skip 2 single crochet, repeat from * and close the row. Finish. Crochet a second foot in the same way and sew both to the bottom of the body.
Crochet a hanging loop using a single strand of blue yarn. Make a chain of 31 stitches and work back across it 30 single crochet to make the chain. Sew the chain to the top of the head.

Crocheting circles

A circle can begin with a crocheted chain of stitches. Crochet a couple of chain stitches and close it with a slip stitch into a circle; see illustration K 1, 2, 3. Now, various types of stitches can be worked in this ring. Begin with a chain to make a row of single crochet stitches and then crochet in the ring; work single crochet across the chain stitches until the ring is filled. Close the row with a slip stitch in the chain; see illustration K 4, 5. You can continue to work in single crochet stitches, beginning each row with a chain stitch and closing with a slip stitch in the first chain. You must increase at a regular rate if the circle is to stay flat. There are no absolute rules but usually you'll find the following instructions will work. In the first row crochet 2 stitches in every stitch, in the following row 2 stitches in every 2nd stitch, in the next row 2 stitches in every 3rd stitch, and so forth. In this way the number of stitches added is the same in every row and the increases come right above each other with 1 stitch more between the increases every row. This method of increasing can, occasionally, turn out to be too rapid so check your work by placing it on a table. If it begins to ripple you must increase more slowly for example by working 1 row with increasing and 1 row without. If the work begins to roll back on itself, more increases per row are required.

Spiral crocheting

In spiral crocheting only the starting chain is closed into a ring. After that the rows are crocheted continuously without closing each row with a slip stitch. However, because the size of the circle must be increased regularly, it is recommended that you mark the beginning of the row with a colored thread. Place this thread between the stitches at the beginning of the row. If the crochet is heavy you should work the thread in at every row; with finer crochet work you can do this every 3rd row. This thread acts as a marker and is visible on both the right and the wrong sides of your work. Remove the thread when the crochet work is finished. In crocheting in a spiral don't make the increases directly above each other but, rather divide them among the stitches of the row.

A loop to start

Make a loop as in beginning to crochet; see illustration K 6 and 7. Crochet single crochet in the ring (see illustration 8), closing the row with a slip stitch in the first stitch; see illustration 9. Pull the starting thread through firmly so that the loop is closed.

Double crochet in a ring

Close the starting chain with a slip stitch. Work 3 chains for the first double crochet and then work double crochets on the chain; see illustration K 10. Close the row with a slip stitch through the top stitch of the 3 chains; see illustrations K 11 and 12. In crocheting half double crochet begin with 2 chain stitches; in crocheting triple crochet begin with 4 chain stitches.

More dolls

In the picture on page 68 more examples of dolls can be seen made of crocheted rounds.

Crocheted circles were the starting point of the crocheted items in this child's room. The pajama bag on the bed is a variation on the mascot shown on page 65. The dolls on the rug are made from circles as are the designs on the sitting cube.

And because this room is a child's room, primary and secondary colors have been chosen. These colors are very appealing to children and are extremely cheerful.

Give the children a say

The children themselves can decide on the motif for the rug or the sitting cube. Give them circles cut from colored paper and let them design animals or dolls. If a child can draw very well, let him plan the entire design. Circles are made easily by drawing around a saucer or other round object. Naturally, the designs don't have to be made only from circles. Squares and triangles can also be used. Let the child choose the shape himself and bring your own imagination to bear on the stitches and the design of the finishing edge. The instructions for the doll can help you with this.

Some tips

Use a thick, not-too-fluffy yarn for the background yarn for *the rug*. Crochet the rug in single or half double crochet stitches. The designs, which are sewn on, can be crocheted from a thinner yarn. The size is about 24 by 48 inches.

For the *sitting cube* crochet six squares; each can be made in a different color or they can all be made in the same color. Each square should measure 12 by 12 inches. Crochet 1 row of single crochet in the same color around each square and 1 row in a contrasting color which must also work with the next square; in the example this is black. After the designs have been worked out these can be crocheted and sewn to the squares. Sew all the squares to each other except the bottom. Fill the cube with squares of foam rubber or polyurethane, then sew on the bottom.

The pajama bag

The pajama bag is the big sister of the doll on the wall. The diameter of the body is 10 inches and of the head 8 inches. An opening must be crocheted in the body to take the pajamas. For this crochet chains rather than single crochet in a section

A detail from the sitting cube. Each side has a different animal or doll design.

measuring 7 inches. Skip the same number of single crochet in the previous row as you have crocheted chains, then continue in single crochet. In the next row, work single crochet on the chain.
Crochet circles for the hands and feet measuring about 3 inches in diameter and work a decorative edging around them.
Crochet two each of the head and body because the body will hold the pajamas and the head will be filled with a thin layer of foam rubber or polyurethane foam.

Other things to make

Following the example of the sitting cube you can make a *clothing box*. Use cotton yarn for this as it is easier to wash and some children are allergic to wool.
Tidies for toys are very practical. To make one crochet a rectangular piece and then, for the pockets on it, crochet squares with crocheted pictures such as a cat, a train, and the sun. Look in a coloring book for ideas. You can often find in these books designs that can be easily crocheted.
Round or square *cushions* can be decorated with crocheted designs in the same way.
A solid colored *spread* on the child's bed can be decorated with animals, variously colored balls, or other designs.
The great advantage of crochet is that almost any shape can be crocheted.
Make a drawing and crochet according to the drawing. For increasing and decreasing, see the pointers at the back of this book in the stitch glossary. You can see that the further we move in this book the more we move toward creative crochet. This is our intention as them mindless copying of designs does not always give satisfaction. What you bring to the work yourself is often what gives it its character.

The possibilities of the pentagon

Crochet 3 chains, turn and crochet 2 single crochet in the 3rd chain from the hook. Turn with 2 chains, crochet in each of the following 2 single crochet 1 single crochet and work 2 single crochet on the last single crochet. Turn with 2 chains, crochet across in single crochet making 2 single crochet in the last stitch. Continue in this way until there are 21 single crochet. Increase by 1 stitch each side of every row. Turn with 2 chains and crochet 19 single crochet, turn with 2 chains and crochet 18 single crochet. By doing this, you are decreasing. Continue in this way until there are 11 single crochet remaining. The pentagon is finished. Crochet 12 pentagons, crochet a row of single crochet around each pentagon, and sew these together. Before the last seam is closed, stuff with pieces of foam rubber or polyurethane. You have made a ball. You may want to put a bell inside a cardboard box and then inside the ball when stuffing.

9 The Teenager's Room

The teenager's room can certainly not be left out of this book. It is often a cozy cave where many hours are spent playing records, reading, studying, puttering, and talking. Teenagers usually take care of the walls themselves, covering them suitably with such things as posters and vacation souvenirs which, after a few months, disappear to be replaced by new ideas.

The edge of the bed or cushions on the ground are the favorite sitting places for teenagers while listening to records. What about a large round hassock? If the room is relatively small this could be kept under the bed and brought out as a sitting place when there are visitors.

Such a hassock is not difficult to make. In the previous chapter you will find complete information on crocheting circles. The top and bottom of the hassock are crocheted in circles, either by closing rows or by working in spiral fashion. We worked the hassock in rug yarn, but other yarns can be used provided they are smooth; loosely spun yarn tends to shed.

The height of the hassock is determined by the strip of crochet which is sewn between the two circles. Make a chain as long as you want the hassock to be high and crochet in single crochet until the strip measures the circumference of the circle. For stuffing, you will probably have the best results with foam rubber or polyurethane foam slabs. You can also cut up an old foam rubber or polyurethane foam mattress into circles. There are, naturally, also other stuffing materials such as old stockings or cotton batting. If you use these materials, first make an inner cushion of thin cotton to keep the stuffing firmly together. An old leather hassock can be covered with crochet, too, of course.

If you wish, you can decorate the top of the hassock with a design.

Shephard's stitch

Shephard's stitch is named for the shepherd who wandered over the hills while tending his sheep and kept his hands busy by making a pair of mittens or a hat from spun wool. Handspun wool is excellent for this stitch. A smooth wool or other yarn, without bumps and irregularities, is never as effective as the handspun. Shephard's stitch is crocheted in spiral fashion with a thick crochet hook.

By covering an empty potato chip or pretzel can with a slip cover made from handspun wool you can create a delightful container for newspapers, umbrellas, or such things as tennis raquets and hockey sticks.

How to

Crochet very loosely a chain of stitches and close this into a ring with a slip stitch. Continue to crochet in the round. Crochet in spiral fashion a few rows in slip stitches, picking up both loops of the previous row. After that, continue to crochet in slip stitches only picking up the *back* loop of the stitch. Pull each stitch up high. If you don't your work will be too tight. You only need to crochet a cylindar as a bottom is not necessary for this cover. For the last two rows, use both loops of the previous stitch again.

IDEE-LP

Afghan stitch

This crochet technique differs from ordinary crochet. It is worked with a long hook on which there is a hook at one end and a knob, such as is found on knitting needles, at the other.

Afghan stitch is used mainly for flat pieces of work and gives a very sturdy structure. It looks somewhat like both knitting and weaving.

The afghan stitch consists of rows which go back and forth. Just as in the case of knitting all stitches are held on the hook and are worked back and forth. There are many variations possible using this stitch. See page 74 where there are clear drawings showing you the stitches.

Afghan stitch shoulder bag

The combination of unusual yarn and the afghan stitch gives the impression that the bag illustrated is woven.

Begin with a chain of stitches about 10 to 12 inches long. Crochet on this in ordinary afghan stitch until you have a length of 24 inches.

Fold the fabric in half and crochet the sides closed with a row of slip stitches.

Knot fringe along the bottom. For this, use 6 strands of yarn about 6 inches long. Place the yarn, doubled, around the knob of the hook after the hook has been pushed through the bottom row of stitches of the bag. Draw the loop through and pull the end of the bunch of yarn through the loop.

The carrying handle can be made from three bunches of yarn or it can be crocheted. You can make a simple chain of double crochet as described in the chapter on decorative room dividers. You can also make a handle by working several rows of single crochet on a long chain of stitches. Add a tassel at each end.

A flap on the bag

Would you like to have a flap on the bag? In that case, crochet the piece of fabric longer – about 4 inches longer – and let this section come over the double fold. Crochet a row of single crochet around this flap with a loop of chain stitches in the middle. Sew a button on the bag at the same level as the loop. The bag can be lined with a piece of fabric the same color as the yarn, and makes a splendid gift.

Afghan stitch

Begin by crocheting a chain of stitches.

1 Put the needle in the 2nd chain from the hook, pull up a loop, put the needle in the following stitch and pull up another loop; there are now 3 loops on the needle. Continue in this way until all the loops are on the needle.

2 Wrap the yarn around the hook and put this through the first loop.

3 Wrap the yarn around the hook and put this through 2 loops. Continue in this way until all the loops from the hook have been worked; in other words, pull the yarn again and again through 2 loops.

4 Put the hook through the vertical loop and pull the thread through this loop. Put the hook through the next vertical loop and again pull a loop through.

5 Continue in this way until the end of the row.

At the end of this row all the stitches will once again be on the hook. Crochet back in the way described in point 3. Repeat over and over the last 2 rows described.

Variations

Double afghan stitch

Crochet the first two rows as in ordinary afghan stitch; that is, do the two rows after the beginning chain as described under afghan stitch. *Next row:* 1 chain, * wrap the yarn around the hook, put the hook through the vertical loop of the following stitch and pull a loop up. Wrap the yarn around the hook and bind off 2 loops, repeat from *. At the end of the row all the stitches are once again on the hook. Crochet back as in ordinary afghan stitch. Repeat again and again these two rows.

Give crochet a knit effect

Crochet the first 2 rows as in ordinary afghan stitch. In all the odd rows following put the hook through the vertical stitch of

If your teenager is crazy about the guitar, why not crochet one? Make a crocheted bag for your daughter in afghan stitch and give the tennis racquet holder a shepherd's stitch jacket.

Illustration 1 through 5; the afghan stitch. An extra long crochet hook is needed for this.

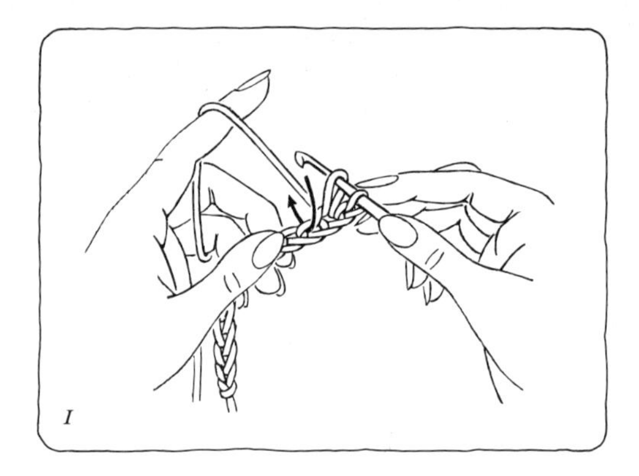

1

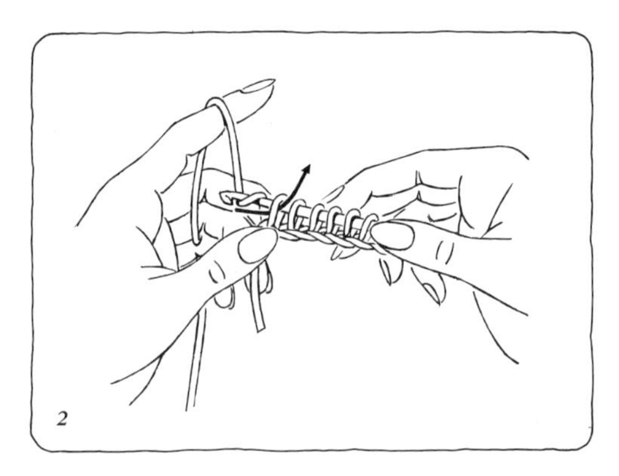

2

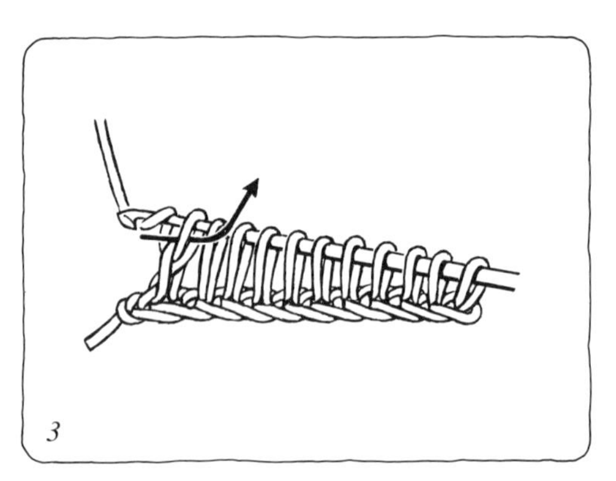

3

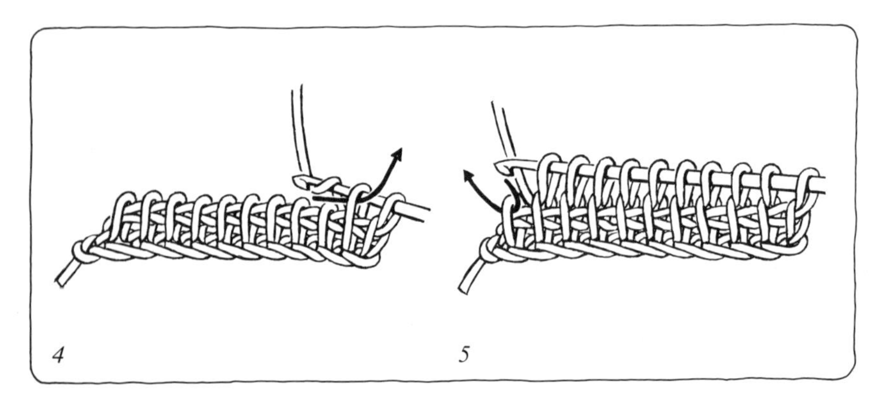

4 5

the previous row so that the horizontal stitch in this vertical stitch is brought to the top on the needle. Wrap yarn around the needle and pull this through.

Wall decoration

What do you think of this wall decoration for a musical teenager?

The phonograph record is crocheted in spirals and, in order to depict the grooves of the record, the single crochets are worked in the back loop of the stitches of the previous row. The label is crocheted separately and joined to the record with chain stitches that go through both layers.

The guitar is based on a pattern so the crocheter can work according to a plan. Redraw the small schematic drawing to the size you want the guitar to be, if you wish. Of course, if there is a guitar in the house this can be used as your model.

You can work out for yourself exactly how you want to plan your crochet stitches for this guitar.

The sounding board and the neck of the guitar are made from lightweight wood, such as balsam, and the strings are crocheted chains.

After the guitar is placed on the phonograph record, some kind of support must be placed on the back of the record. This can, for example, be a piece of hardboard glued to the back or stapled to it. A sturdy piece of wood is needed which should be the same size and shape as the record as otherwise the crocheted record would fold down on itself when it was hung.

Some geometric forms

In addition to circles and squares, crochet can also be done in the shape of *ovals and triangles.*

For an oval, crochet a chain of 4 or more stitches. Around this chain work one row of single crochet. After the chain crochet the first single crochet in the 2nd stitch from the hook and, at the end of the chain, crochet further along the bottom of the chain. From there work 3 single crochet in 1 stitch at the beginning and end of the chain. Now continue to work around, increasing 2 stitches

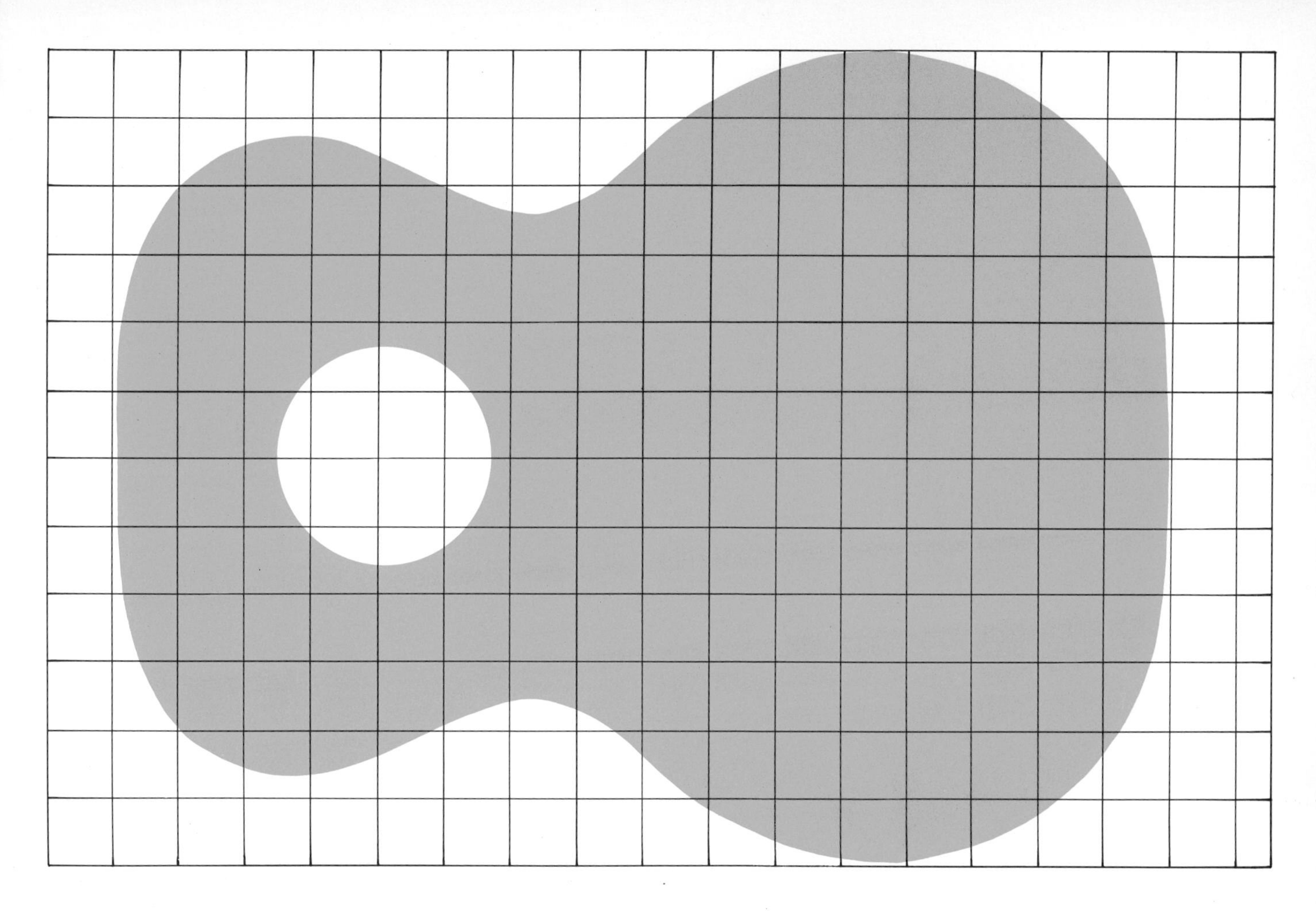

Enlarge this pattern of the guitar to the size you want and then crochet following the pattern.

at the beginning and end of the chain. Do not increase on the sides as you do not want your crochet to grow wider there.

A hexagon

Begin with a chain of 3 stitches and close this into a ring with a slip stitch. Crochet 6 single crochet in this ring and in the following row crochet 2 stitches in every stitch. There are now 12 stitches. In every following row increase 6 stitches, making these increases directly above each other.

A square

Begin as for the hexagon, but this time crochet 4 stitches in the ring. Increase in the following rows 2 stitches in each of the 4 corner stitches by crocheting 3 stitches in 1 stitch. In every following row there will be 2 more stitches between the increases.

10 Free Crochet

Crochet is a simple technique but true works of art can be made with it. Just as a sculptor or painter can give form to his materials, a crocheter can give form and depth to crochet work.
In this type of crochet you can indulge yourself and give free rein to your imagination, whether you are making a wall decoration or something which will stand on its own.
The materials you use – rope, wool, raffia, or whatever – gains form, structure, and meaning by being worked in different crochet techniques.
More and more crocheted art objects are being seen on exhibit in galleries. Crochet is a technique that brings a fabric into being, a fabric that is an art form in itself and not only something limited to clothing, curtains, and other useful objects. More experimentation is being made today, increasing the importance of crochet as an art form.

Crochet knows no frontiers because all of us can go further and bring to the work additional depth.
We are seeing more and more interest today in three-dimensional objects to be hung in space. You can make delightful things of this kind in crochet work. Often the beginning of working in crochet as an art form is very simple, but with time the crocheter develops more and more. Some preparations should be made before the starting chain is worked. The potter, the painter, the sculptor, all make a sketch before beginning. This must also be done by the person working in crochet as an art form.

'The Woods' as an example

For this work I started with a drawing. Don't be alarmed – by this I don't mean a complete drawing but rather a sketch showing the ground, the tree trunks, and the closed tree tops above. The width and the height were given a definite size but not the thickness of the trunks although the number of trunks was included in order to get a good joining of the ground with the tops of the trees.
Next, using a felt pen, I indicated colors and, here and there, a knot or opening.

The next step

The next step is the searching out of the colors and the yarns. Once you have decided what the theme of the crochet work is to be, look for suitable colors. Get together all kinds of yarn and thread. If all the colors you want are not available, it is very simple to dye them yourself. For the wall piece I dyed wool and rope in colors that were missing in my collection of yarns.
There are many ways *to dye yarn*. It can be done with synthetic dyes which are available in most ten cent stores in small packages or you can use natural products such as henna, shells of nuts, or onions. Many books have been written on this subject. If the yarns must be dyed shades of green, begin with the lighter shade; the color becomes darker as more dye powder is added or if you let the yarns stand a long time in the dye bath. Different colors of dye mixed together can often give good results as do different fibers combined in the same dye bath. Each fiber comes out in a different shade.

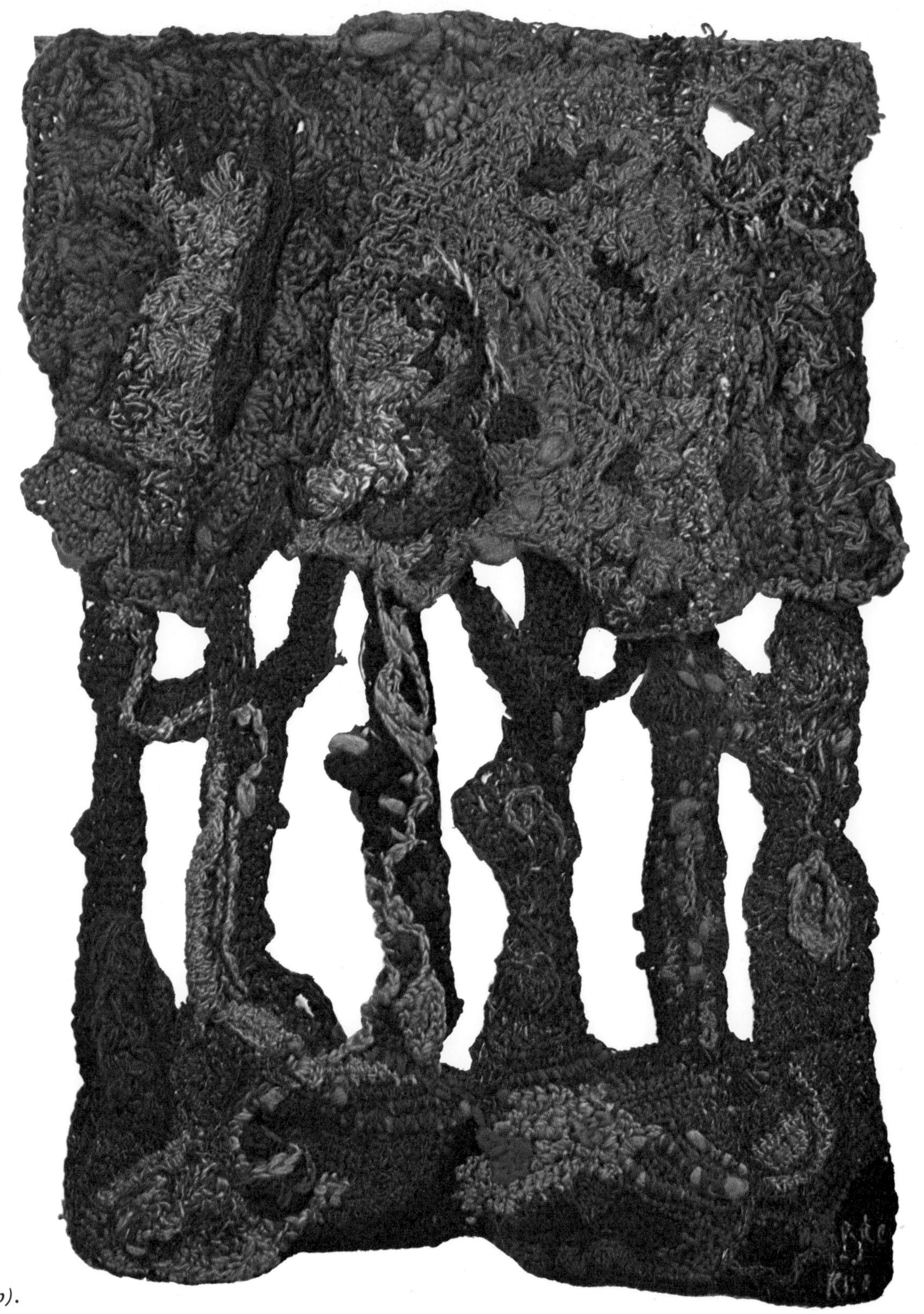

The woods (Rite van der Klip).

Closing rows worked in the round. After each round the work is turned.

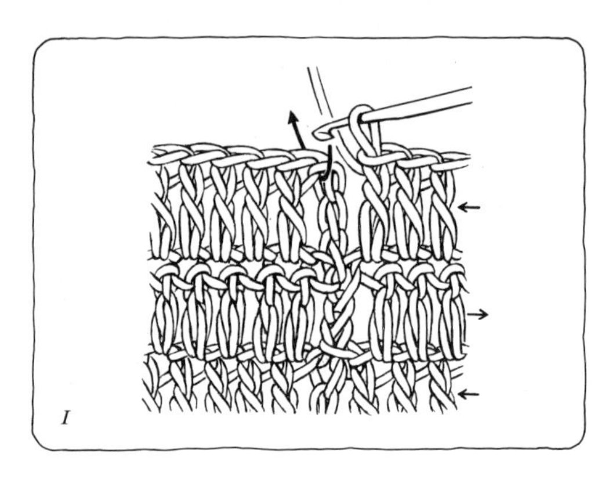
1

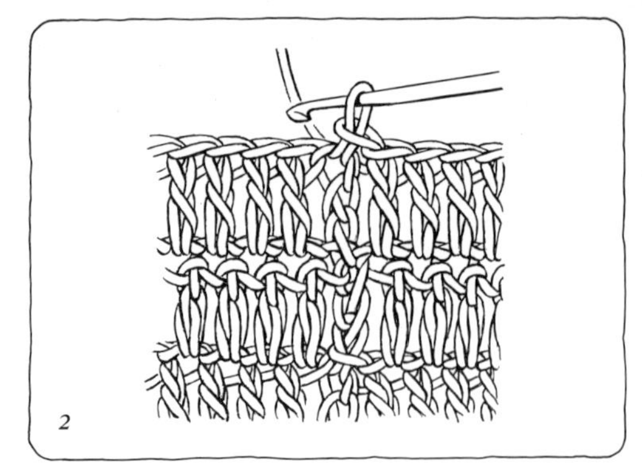
2

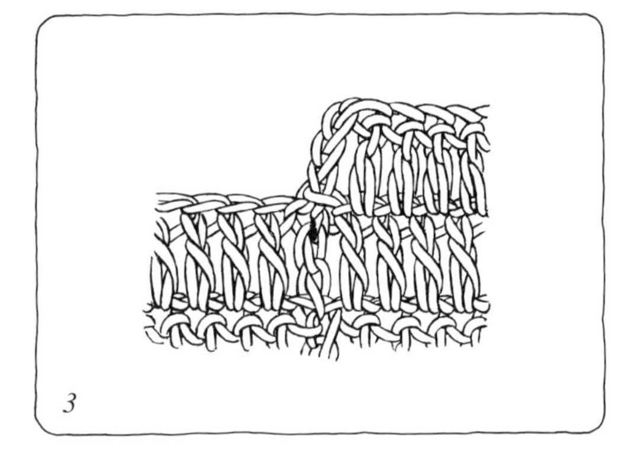
3

Thick and thin
Not only different thicknesses of yarns are needed for a crocheted work of art but also different sizes of crochet hooks. You don't have to always use thin yarn with a fine crochet hook; a thick hook used with thin yarn, for instance, gives the stitch a looser character and a very interesting effect. Experiment with different yarns and different hooks to discover their possibilities.

Where to begin
Always begin with the background, the basic shape of the piece of work. This can be crocheted in a simple stitch – what stitch depends on the art work itself. The woods, where the roots of the trees were crocheted later, required a quite heavy structure and I used rather stiff yarns in dark colors. For dimension, some whimsical stitches such as popcorn stitches and clusters were used. The trunks were worked when this area was completed.

Continuing
Once this background has been worked out you can continue to build up the design as you wish. In the case of the trunks, you can crochet them in anyway you want. Once the trunks are firmly in place, you can add the leaves to the trees. Keep in mind that every type of tree found in nature has its own leaves and coloring. Keep your work from being too massive by leaving some spaces empty. For the tops of the trees scallops work well but so do popcorn stitches and double crochets and large picots and many other stitches.

Study your work
Put the crochet work down now and then as you work on it and study it from a distance to see if it is coming out the way you want it. You can often see things better from a distance. Correct, change, and embellish the work where necessary. Sometimes just a couple of chain stitches can change the picture to what you want or give more life to a somewhat somber section.

More examples
Crochet a rectangular piece of fabric in a basic color and divide it irregularly. On the top of each area crochet a row of heavy chain stitches in another color. On this row of chain stitches you can work garlands of chain stitches or chains with half double crochet, working so that the chains hang down. At the end of these chains work a cylindar or another shape. By working with many different colors a vibrant wall hanging can be developed in this way.
Another idea is to crochet arches with a width of about 2 inches in various colors

and stitches. The arches can be U shaped or part of a half circle. If you braid these sections together you can make a whimsical wall hanging.

Crocheting cylindars

Crocheting cylindars starts with the crocheting of a ring of a chain of stitches. Close the chain with a slip stitch and crochet on this chain *without* increasing, closing every row. You can also work a spiral or close every row with a slip stitch and then crochet back. This crocheting backward and forward in the round gives a work a different structure from that resulting when it is worked entirely in the round. The illustrations 1, 2, and 3 show this. The illustrated crochet stitches are double crochet.

If you want to give the cylindar a slant, then you can increase on one side of the ring and decrease on the opposite side so that the number of stitches remains the same. This can also be done with shortened rows. To do this, crochet half the number of stitches in the row, turn, crochet 1 chain, skip 1 stitch, and crochet back to the beginning. Turn again, crochet a stitch, and skip the following stitch. Now crochet across all the stitches of the row. By repeating these last 2 rows a couple of times a slant will develop in the cylindar. Still another way of developing the slant is, if the cylindar is worked in single crochet, work double crochet in place of single crochet on one side so that side becomes higher than the other. If the cylindar is being crocheted in double crochet, you can get the same effect by crocheting single crochet or slip stitches on half of every row.

Bulging tubes

Crochet as for a cylindar and, where you wish, work 3 increases in 1 stitch. After 2 or more rows decrease by the number of stitches you have increased. By doing this 3 or 4 times, placing the stitches next to each other, you will create a bulge. Decrease by these stitches, too, after a few rows. Many shapes can be crocheted in this manner. By starting with a cylindar and letting your crochet grow out from that, thickening it and thinning it, you can make a long snake which, turned back on itself, can make a splendid object to hang in space.

Free design

The design shown on page 80 is built up of crocheted saucer shapes, worked on rings of various sizes. Work single crochet on the rings, increasing here and there. When the edge is about 2 inches wide, decrease until the circle is closed. Link the saucer shapes together with crocheted chains and you have an object suitable for hanging. Stiffenings in the crochet work are often necessary for similar pieces of art.

Filling and stiffening

Stiffening can be used in crochet work at any time to give a visible shape, as in the case of the rings, or as a filling in of the shape.

You can find materials to give the work body anywhere. Use fine wire netting, foam rubber or polyurethane foam cut in pieces, or even plastic clothesline. You will be surprised at the variety of things you can use. You can work the crochet directly on the stiffening material or make it first to shape and then add the stiffening.

Crocheters, like the makers of stuffed wall hangings, should make a point of collecting everything as there will always be a piece of work each item can be used in.

A filling material is especially necessary in the case of the three dimensional crocheted pieces to give these the right form. The stuffing material depends upon the material from which the object is crocheted; if this is rope or another stiff fiber the stuffing should be stiff, too, such as fine wire. If the yarn is soft and the crochet work is supple, then use a soft filling material, such as flakes of foam rubber or polyurethane, kapok, cotton batting, or pieces of thin fabric. Don't forget to use old nylon stockings and panty hose.

Nylon stockings can be cut in spiral fashion and dyed, making them useful rags with which you can crochet. You can also crochet with a thin rope of another fabric.

Mobile by Lieke Smulders.

Shaping consisting of;
1 slip stitch
1 single crochet
1 half double crochet
1 double crochet
1 triple crochet
1 double triple crochet

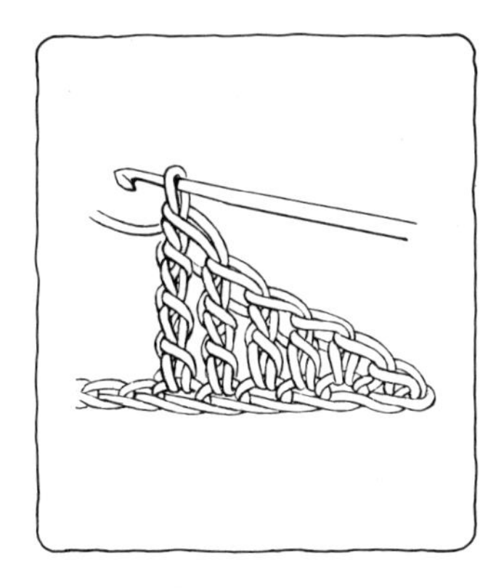

Crocheting in two colors; the thread not being worked is carried along in the row.

Wall hanging

It is necessary to sew a lining to the back of a crocheted wall hanging. If the edges sag somewhat, you can sew on the back against the crochet a piece of fabric cut on the straight of the grain.

The wall hanging can either be hung by means of a dowel or be stretched in a wooden frame. Don't stretch it too forcefully; the crochet work must keep its supple character.

The freedom of crochet

With crochet you can, if you are fast and use coarse materials, make in a day a piece of work. You are not bound to a definite canvas. There are no rules such as exist for fine embroidery or dressmaking. Crochet gives everyone a freedom that can be used infinitely and it can be worked in a relaxed way. The work is stimulating and, influenced by the imagination and the creative sense, each work is a new experience. The shape plays no demanding role. The colors are important, but you have more freedom in using them than in, for instance, planning curtains for a room.

You may feel that free crochet is not for you, that you just don't have the necessary talent. Naturally, the first piece of work you do will not be exactly what you would like, but you can always take out a section or add a section until you are more pleased. Once you have succeeded with this form the pieces will become better and better and you will find your own resourcefulness growing. Don't throw that first thing you make away; keep it carefully as you may find later that it has elements that inspire you in more advanced work.

Train your eye by going to exhibits in galleries and museums; you will find you can always pick up new ideas. Always try to advance yourself in your art.

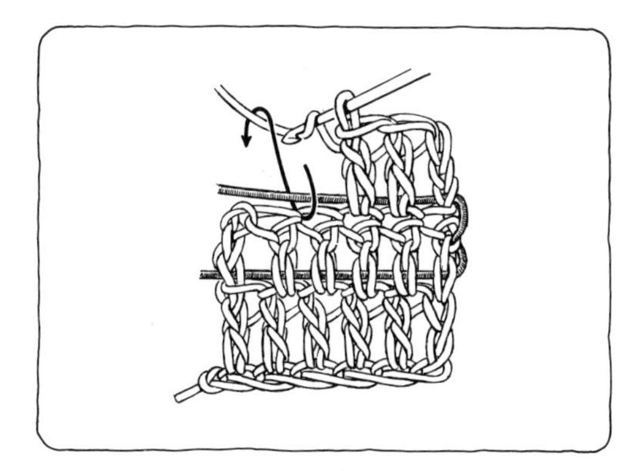

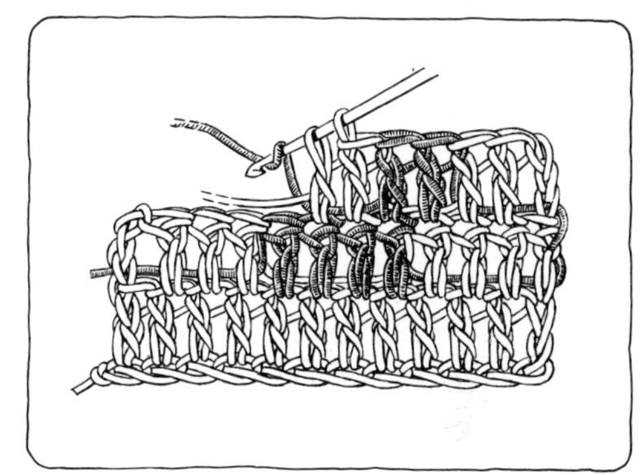

11 Materials and Yarns

Few tools are needed for crochet. One or more crochet hooks are the first thing you should buy.

The numbering

The numbering of crochet hooks is extremely confusing. In many parts of the world crochet hooks follow the sizes of the International Standard Range (abbreviated to ISR). These sizes are in millimeters and begin with the smallest at number 2. They go to number 5 in half steps, such as 3, 3½, 4, 4½. After number 5 these hooks continue to go up in steps of 1 number at a time to 10. There are also larger sizes available.
The International Standard Range is not, however, truly international. Furthermore, for historical reasons, the material from which a crochet hook is made affects its numbering.

Steel crochet hooks

The first crochet hook was probably a home-made wooden one. After that came steel crochet hooks. They were mainly made for crocheting with thin crochet yarns and cotton. The head (hook) of the needle is fairly sharp so that the hook can be pushed easily through fabric if, for instance, you are crocheting a border around a handkerchief or around a linen table-cloth.
Steel crochet hooks are numbered in reverse order of size. That means that size 00 is the largest and size 14 the smallest.

Bone, plastic, and aluminum hooks

These hooks are lettered rather than numbered. The sizes move from B, the smallest that can be found easily, to K, the largest in the aluminum hooks. Plastic hooks usually start at D, rather than B, and go on up to Q. The letters mean the same as they do for aluminum hooks.
Crochet hooks, like knitting needles, were traditionally made of bone. Bone hooks are rarely seen today; the lettering system was the same.
Bone, plastic, and aluminum hooks all have heads which are less sharp than the head on steel hooks.

Afghan hooks

Afghan hooks are made of aluminum or plastic; they are lettered in the same way as regular aluminum or plastic crochet hooks. They look like knitting needles as they have a knob at one end with, of course, a hook at the other end. They are longer than the ordinary crochet hooks as they are used in afghan stitch, a technique in which all the stitches are on the needle while every other row is worked.

Hairpin lace fork

This is available in various forms, all roughly resembling a hairpin. At one time, the forks came in different widths but today they are adjustable. The fork is not, of course, a form of crochet hook but a fork on which crochet is done. You need an ordinary crochet hook, too, to use a hairpin lace fork. It is only used in making hairpin lace.

Other items

Few things in addition to the crochet hooks

are needed. You'll want a pair of scissors, needles with both sharp and blunt points for finishing, a tape measure, and...

Crochet yarns

The conventional crochet yarns include cotton, linen, and wool. Today, the synthetic yarns, and especially acrylic, are also important.

Furthermore, in free crochet when crochet is used to create an art form, other materials can be used including, for instance, copper wire, plastic thread, strips of leather, strips of rags, raffia, all kinds of string, and many other materials.

Cotton yarns

Cotton yarn is one of the traditional crochet yarns and is still extremely popular. In working with a ball of cotton yarn, always start with the end in the center of the ball as it will unwind more smoothly.

Lightweight cotton yarns are usually worked with steel hooks; the heavy rug weight yarn takes a very large crochet hook.

Cotton comes in many colors for crochet, but white and ecru are the traditional favorites.

Wool and synthetic yarns

There is a tremendous choice available to the crocheter in the wool and synthetic yarns. These, of course, are worked with larger crochet hooks than the thin cotton yarns. The weights vary from lightweight, fluffy mohairs to the heavy sturdy rug yarns. These yarns offer the crocheter a tremendous choice in color as well as weight. Each season new colors are added to keep the yarns in step with fashion.

You can find not only solid yarns but also ones which have been dyed in such a way that, when they are crocheted, they give a wonderfully multi-colored effect.

Yarns made from 100% wool are hard to find but can be beautiful. Some natural color wool yarns, handspun, are outstanding.

Don't limit yourself only to those yarns which are labeled as being for crochet. You can use any of the other yarns for your work, sure that you will achieve a good result.

Blended yarns, containing a blend of a synthetic fiber with wool, can be quite satisfactory. Most synthetics lack elasticity on their own; the wool gives them some elasticity.

Raffia

Raffia, available in both natural and synthetic form, gives crochet a certain stiffness which makes it right for crocheting such items as placemats.

Macramé cord

Macramé cord, which comes in glowing colors and has a delightful sheen, makes an excellent crochet yarn. Use it when you want a fairly heavy yarn.

Other yarns

If you are making crocheted artistic forms, you will want to try using all types of string and metal threads, alternating with cotton and wool yarn.

Strips of rags can be used for rugs, wool yarn, of course, can be used for rugs, and rope makes a very dramatic rug. Because rope tends to be stiff to work, wear gloves when crocheting with it to protect your hands.

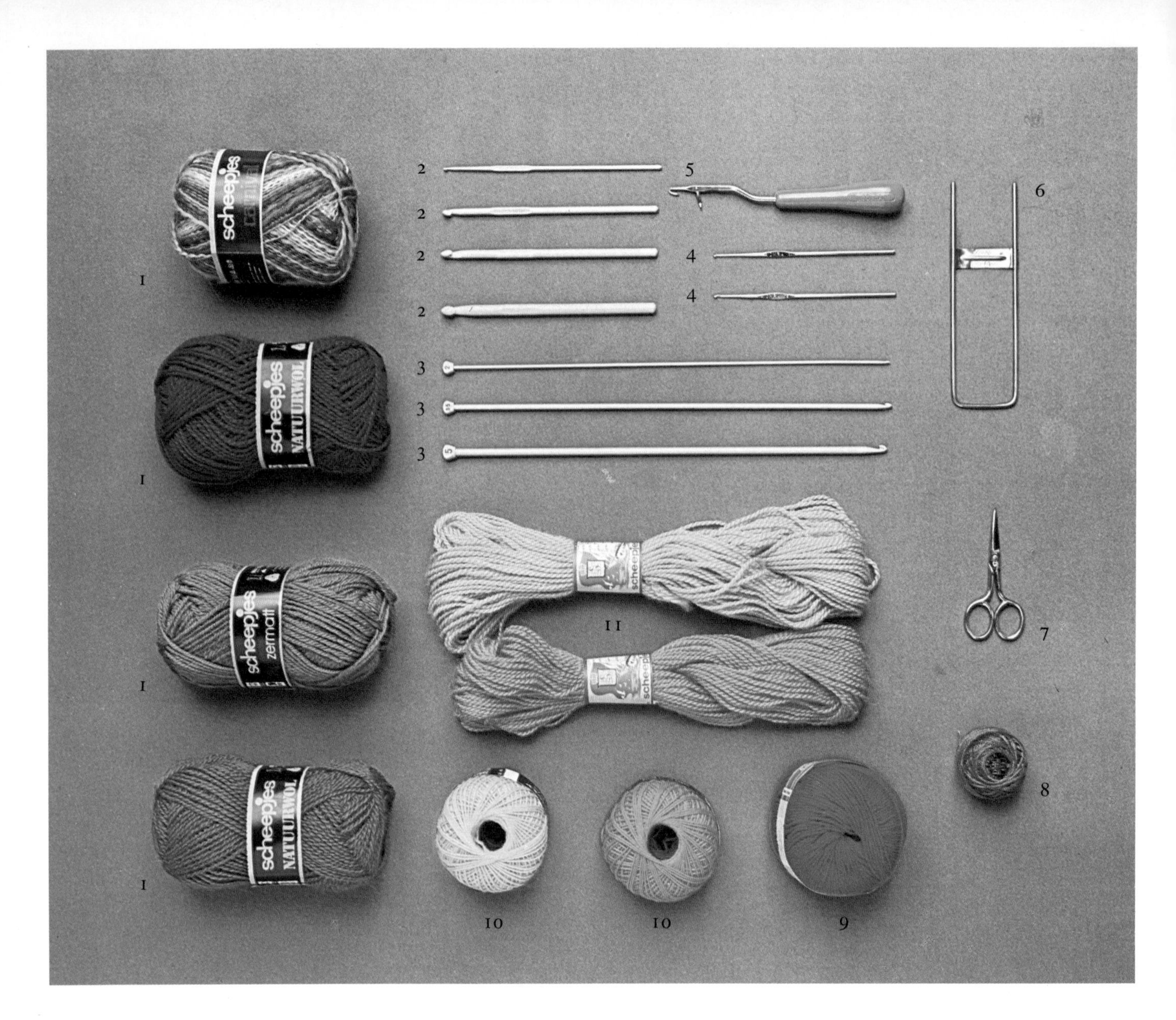

1 various types of wool for crochet
2 crochet hooks
3 afghan crochet hooks
4 steel crochet hooks
5 special hook for making fringe
6 hairpin lace fork
7 scissors
8 perle yarn
9 macramé cord
10 cotton crochet yarns
11 rya yarn

12 Stitch Glossary

Crochet always begins with a chain of stitches. On this chain single crochet, double crochet, or variations on these stitches are made.

The stitches discussed in this glossary are arranged in order of size, that is, according to the height of the stitch.
The slip stitch gives very little height to the work and is used, therefore, for decreasing the number of stitches on the hook and for closing a row.
The single crochet has one additional step and is, therefore, higher.
The half double crochet and the double crochet come next.
You can get additional height by working triple crochet or double triple crochet which require that the yarn be wrapped around the hook additional times.

Chain stitch. See illustrations A and A1.
This is the beginning stitch for all crochet.

Chain stitch

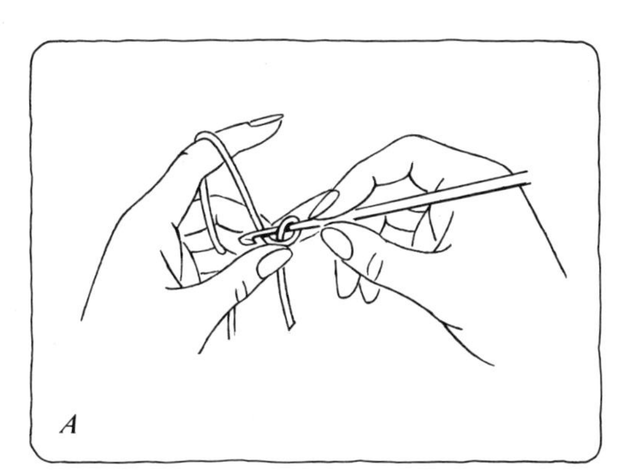

A

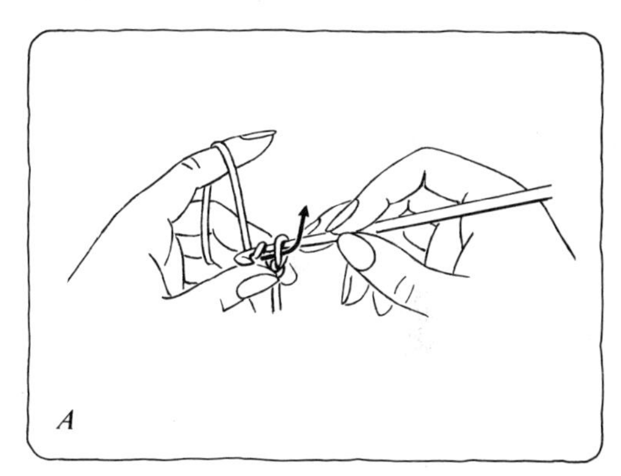

A

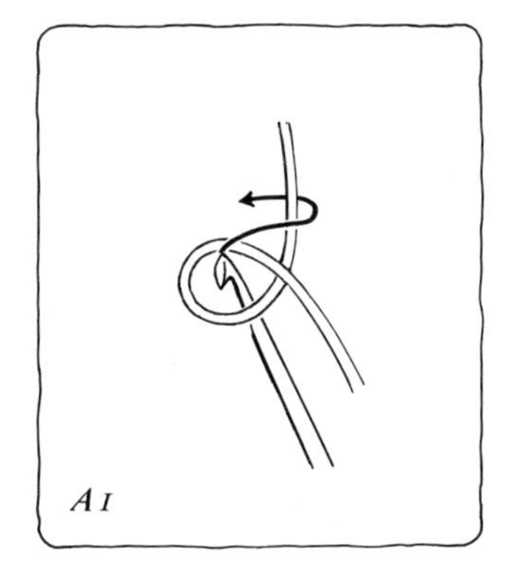

A1

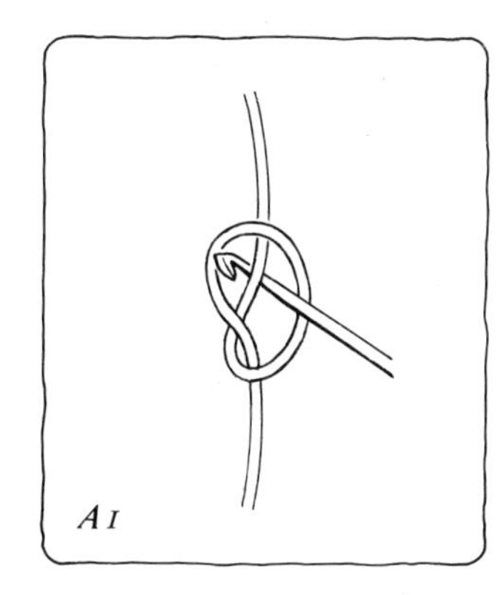

A1

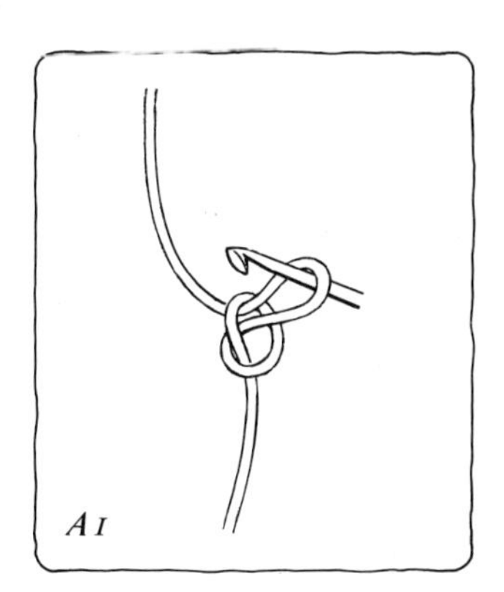

A1

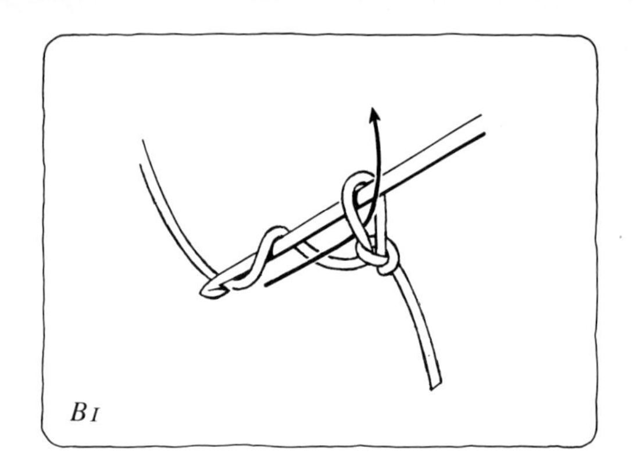

B1

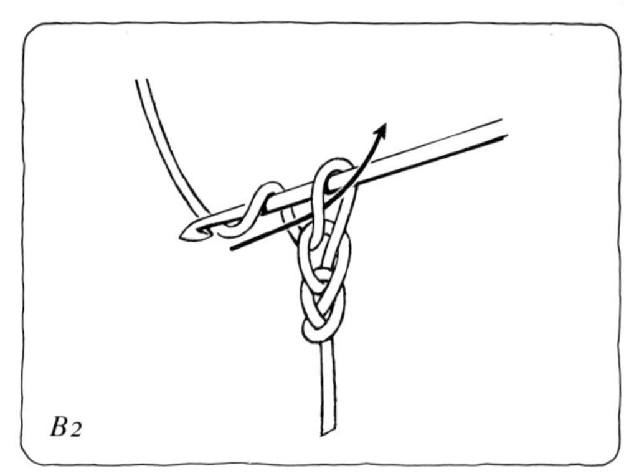

B2

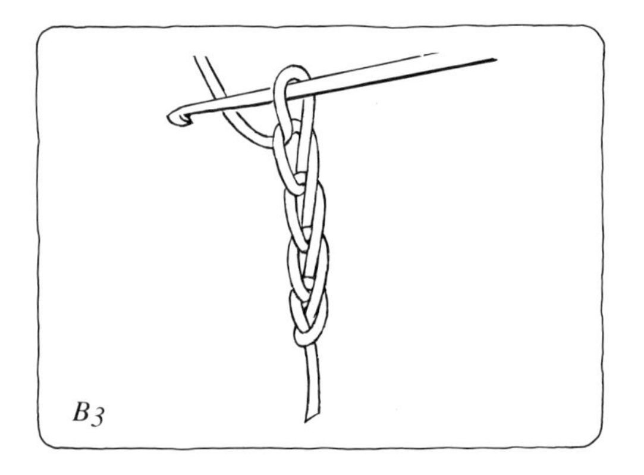

B3

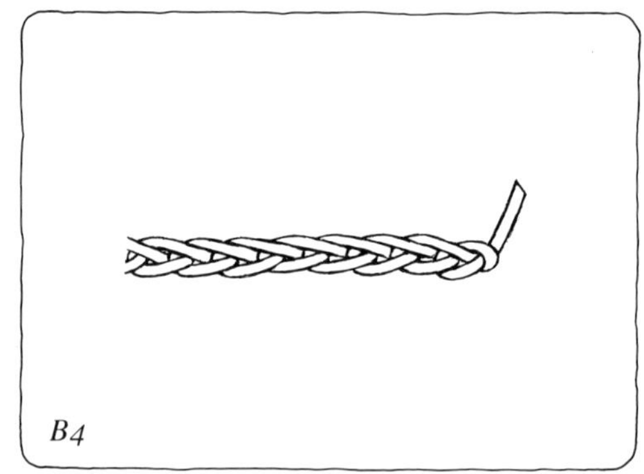

B4

Chain. See illustration B.

Wrap the yarn around the crochet hook and pull this through the loop on the needle.

By repeating these steps you make a chain of stitches. This chain is the basis for all crochet work. The more important basic stitches are all made on a chain.

Slip stitch

Slip stitch, see illustration C number 1, 2, and 3.

1 Put the hook in the 2nd stitch from the hook, catch the yarn with the hook and pull this through the stitch and the loop on the hook.

2 Put the hook in the following stitch and catch the yarn.

C1

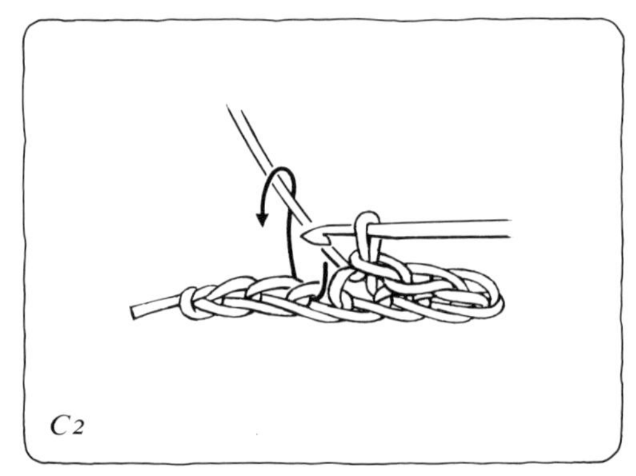

C2

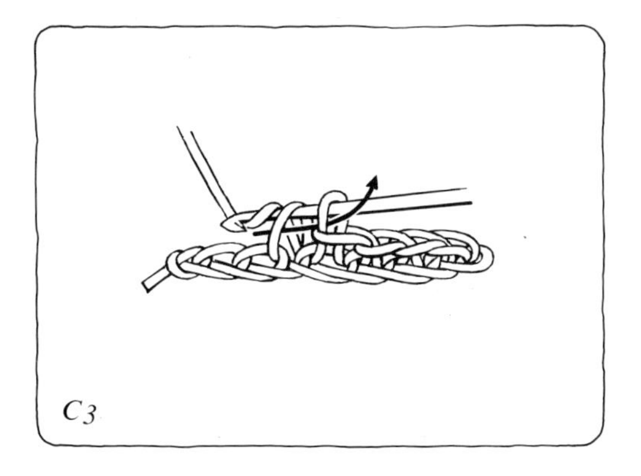

3 Pull this through both loops.

Single crochet

Single crochet. See illustration D, numbers 1 through 8.

1 Put the hook in the 2nd stitch of the chain through both top loops. Wrap the yarn around the hook.
2 Pull this through the stitch; there are now 2 loops on the hook. Wrap the yarn around the hook and pull this through both loops. This is a single crochet.
3 Crochet single crochets in all the other stitches of the chain in the same way.
4 The last stitch is worked in the loop that started the chain. Turn, see arrow.

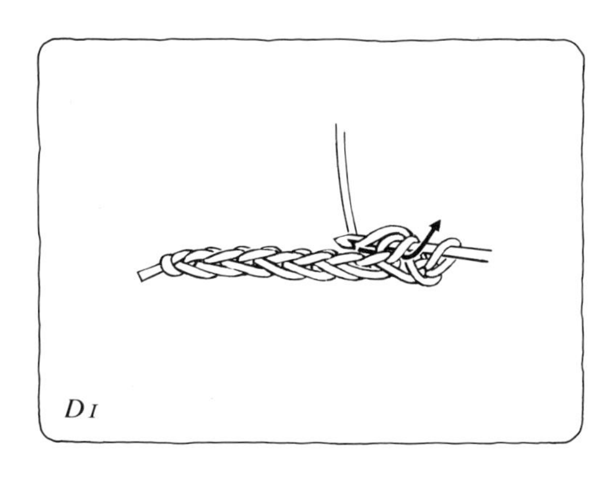

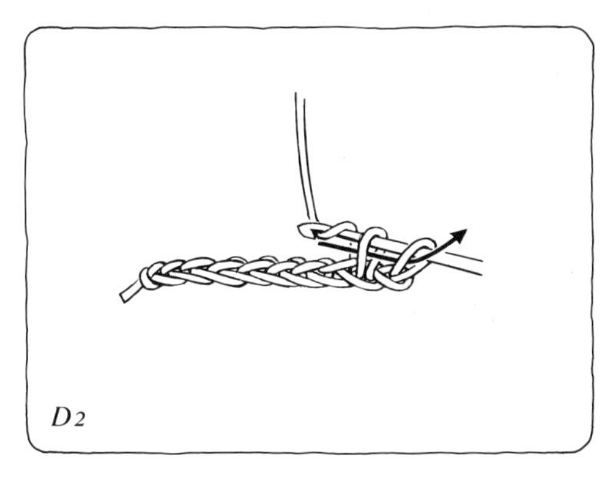

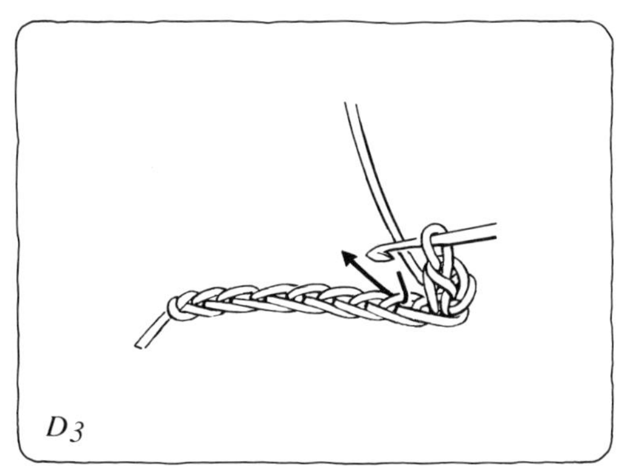

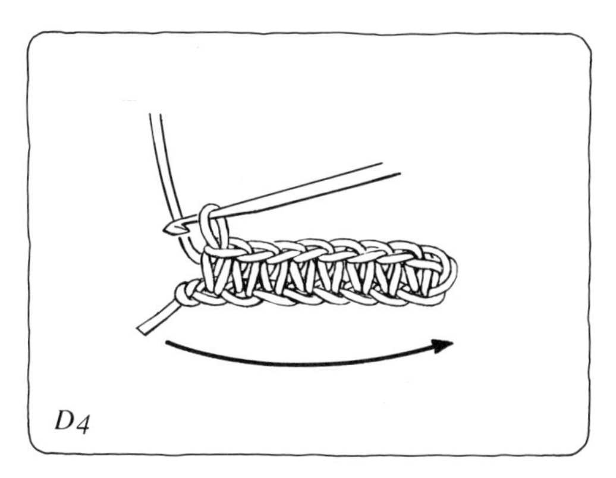

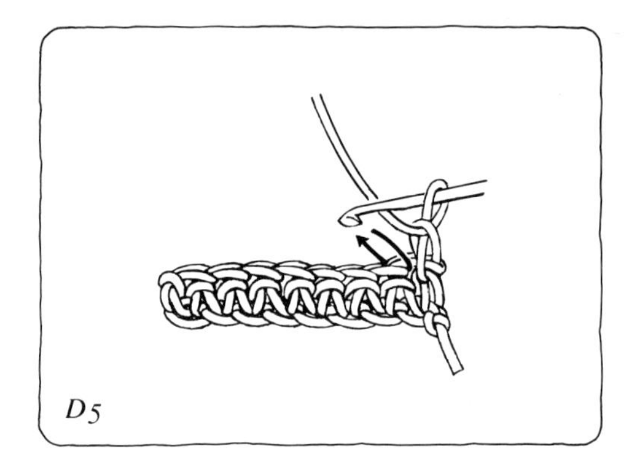

D5

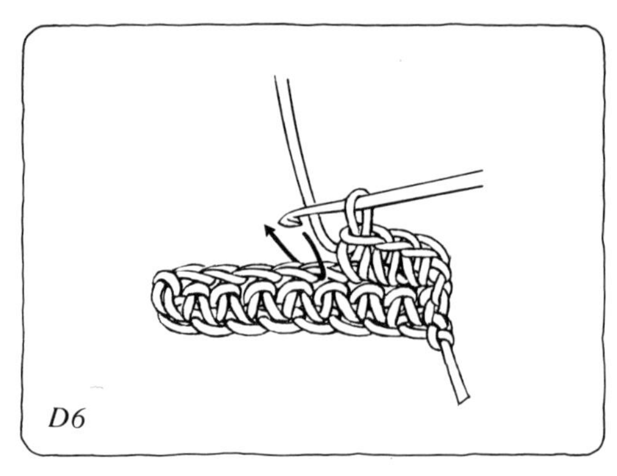

D6

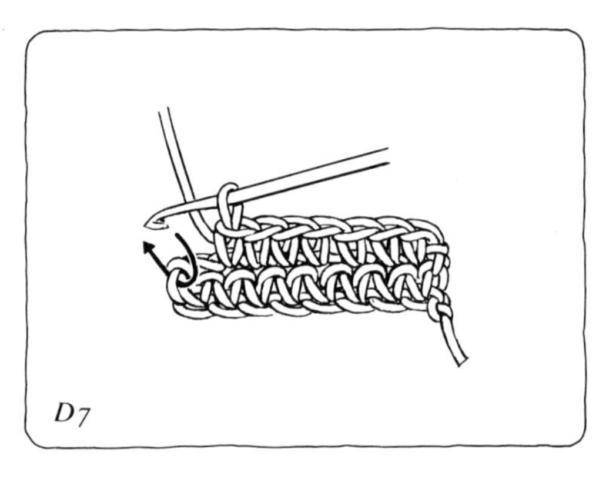

D7

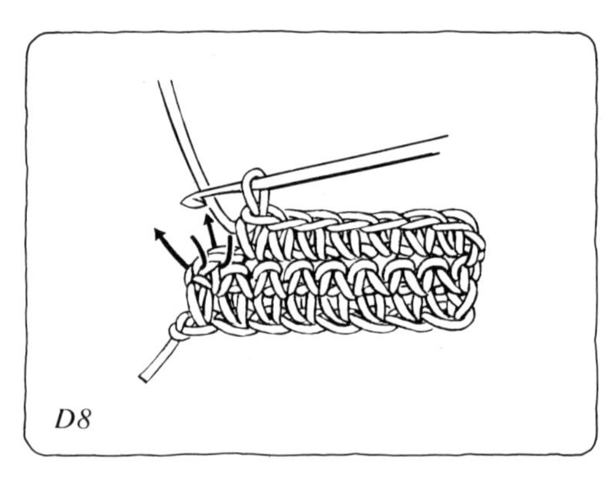

D8

5 Crochet 1 chain to turn; this is the first stitch. Put the hook in the following stitch.
6 Crochet in every following stitch 1 single crochet, putting the hook through both top loops.

7 Crochet the last single crochet in the chain at the end of the row.
8 Turn, crochet 1 chain and then crochet in single crochet. The last single crochet is worked on the chain of the turn of the previous row.

Half double crochet

Half double crochet. See illustration E, number 1 through 8.

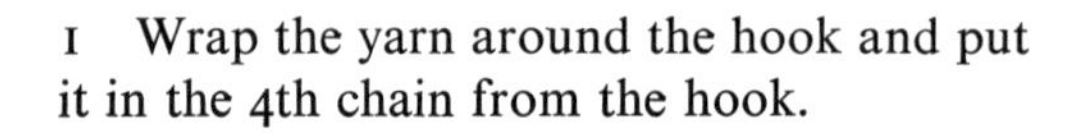

1 Wrap the yarn around the hook and put it in the 4th chain from the hook.

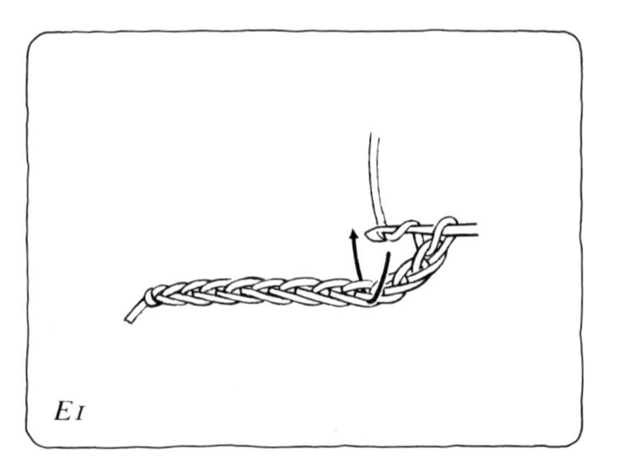

E1

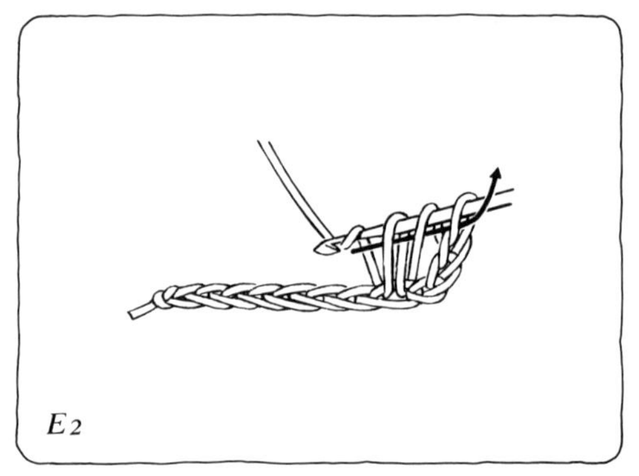

E2

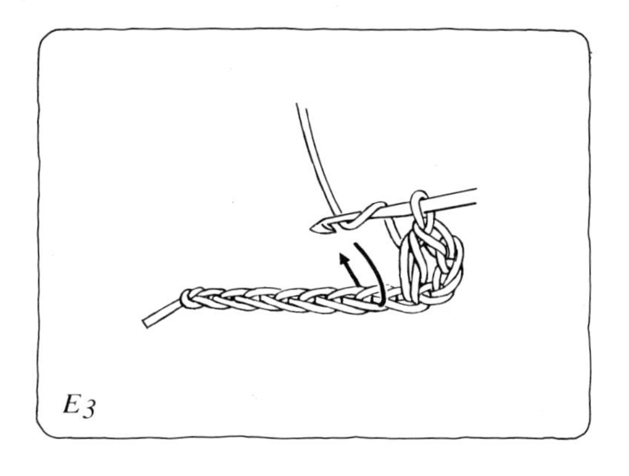

E3

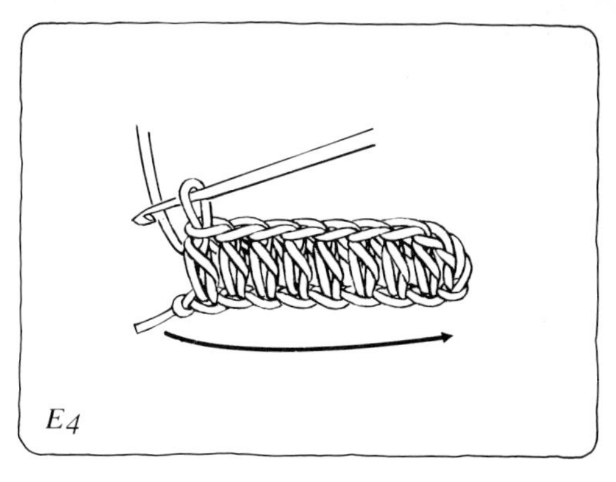

E4

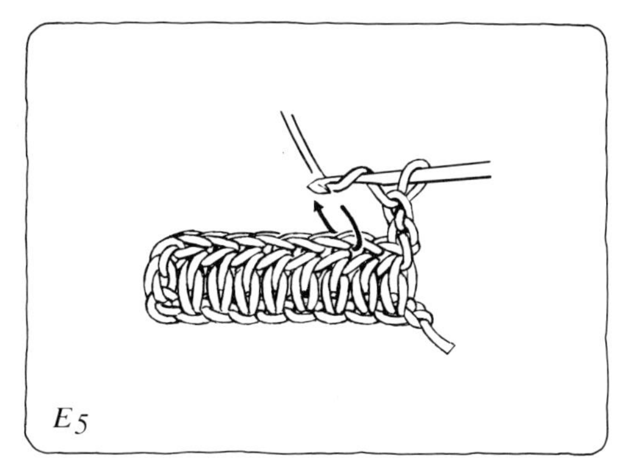

E5

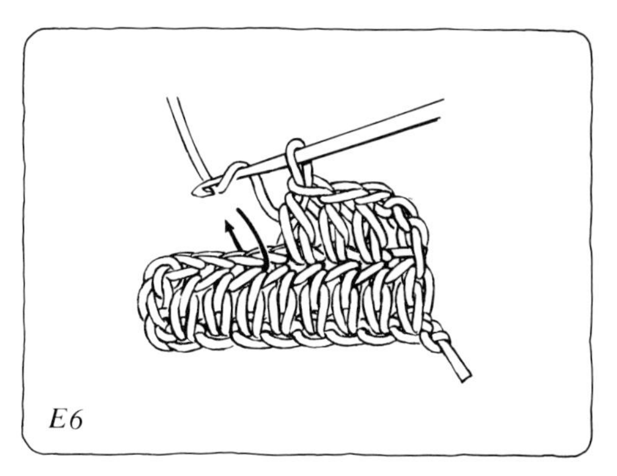

E6

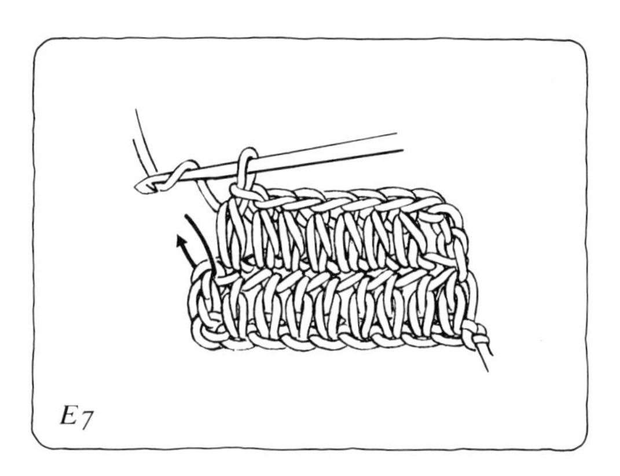

E7

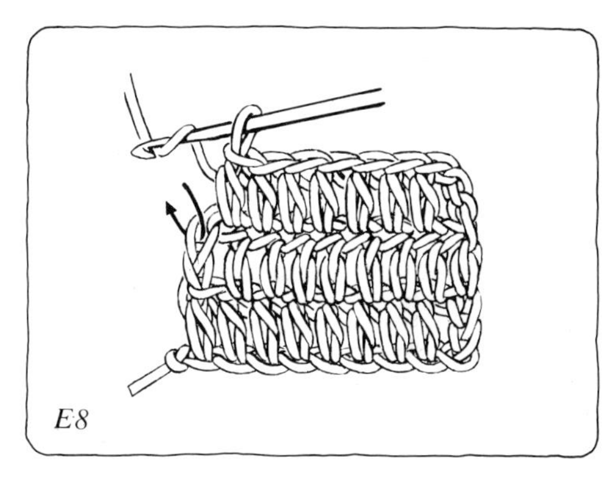

E8

2 Wrap the yarn around the hook, pull this through the stitch and wrap it around again; there are now 3 loops on the hook. Wrap the yarn around the hook again and pull through these 3 loops.
3 Wrap the yarn around the hook again and put the hook in the following stitch.
4 Work half double crochet in this way until the end of the chain and turn.

5 Crochet 2 chains for turning; these count as the first half double crochet stitch in this row. Wrap the yarn around the hook and put the hook through the next stitch.
6 Crochet the row in half double crochet.
7 The last half double crochet is worked at the 2nd chain from the beginning.
8 Turn, crochet 2 chains for the first half double crochet and continue to crochet in half double crochet. The last half double crochet comes at the 2nd chain of the turn.

Double crochet

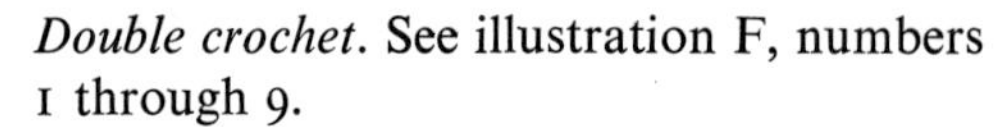

Double crochet. See illustration F, numbers 1 through 9.

1 Wrap the yarn around the hook and put the hook in the 5th chain from the hook.

2 Wrap the yarn around the hook, pull this through the stitch, wrap the yarn around again, and pull this through the 2 loops on the hook.

3 Wrap the yarn around the hook again and pull this through the last 2 loops on the hook.

4 Wrap the yarn around the hook and put the hook through the following stitch.

5 Crochet the row in double crochet to the last stitch and turn; see arrow.

6 Crochet 3 chains for the turn; this is the first double crochet. Wrap the yarn around the hook and put the hook through the next stitch.

7 Crochet the row in double crochet.

8 The last double crochet comes on the 3rd chain from the beginning. Turn.

9 Crochet 3 chains for the first double crochet and crochet the rest of the row in double crochet. The last double crochet comes in the 3rd chain of the turn.

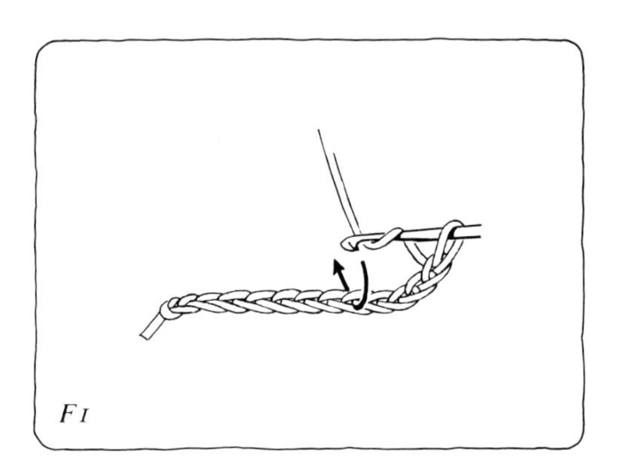

F1

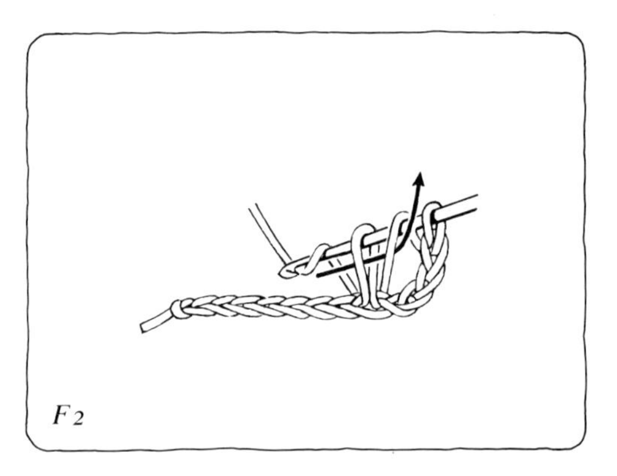

F2

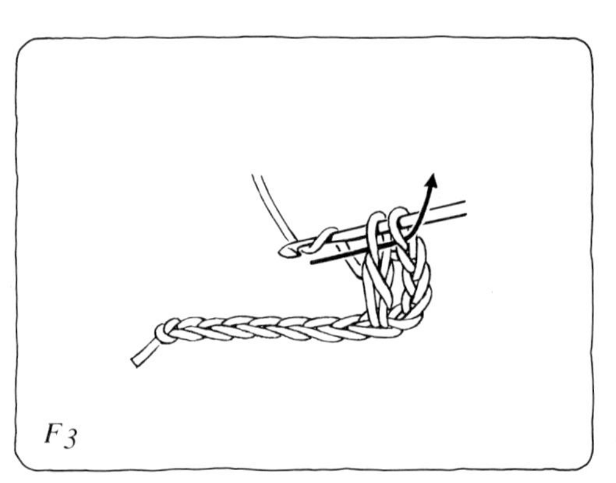

F3

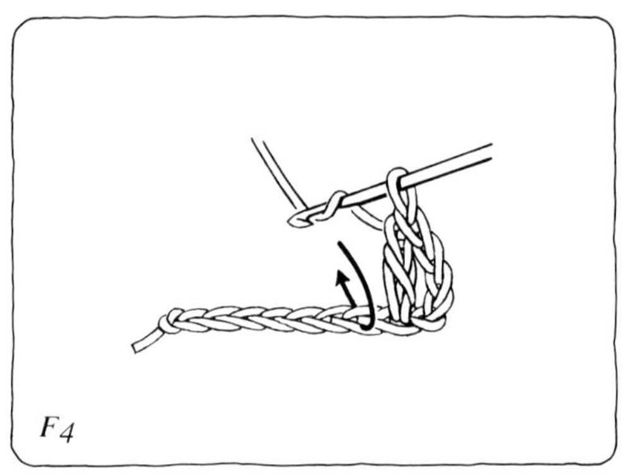

F4

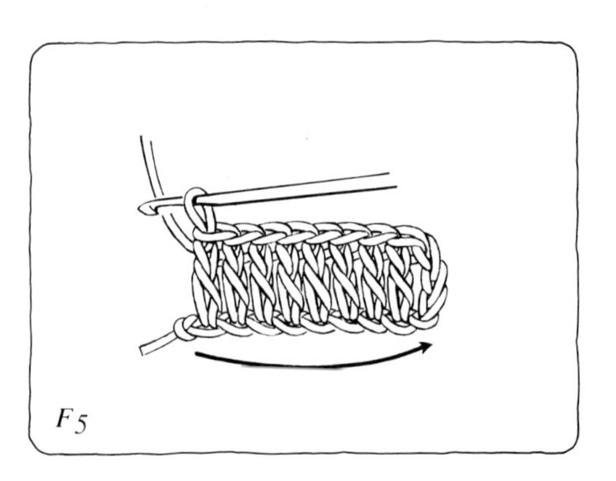

F5

F6

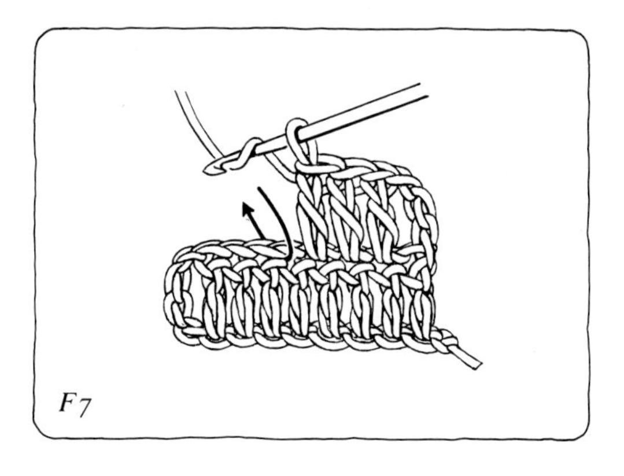

F7

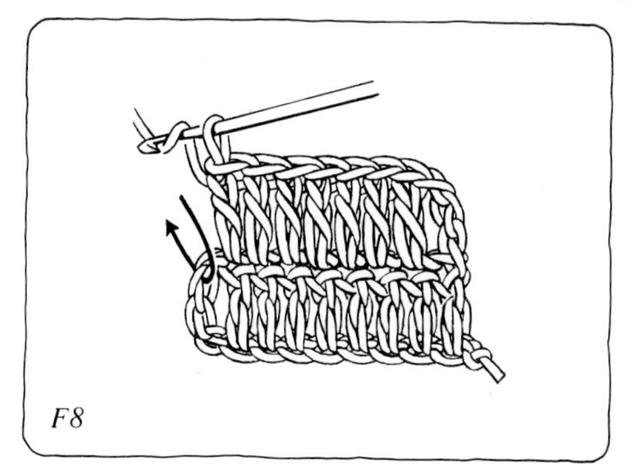

F8

There are other stitches, such as:

Triple crochet. Wrap the yarn around the hook twice, rather than once, but otherwise work as for the double crochet; crochet two loops. Turning with triple crochet is done with 4 chains. Work the first triple crochet in the 6th chain from the hook.

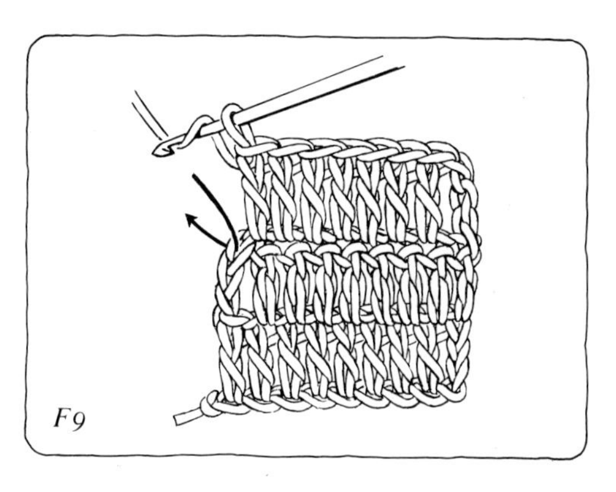

F9

For *double triple crochet* wrap the yarn around the hook 3 times and crochet 5 chains to turn. Start this stitch in the 7th chain from the hook.
All these stitches gain their height from the number of times the yarn is wrapped around the hook. In turning, the number of chains increases by 2 each time the yarn is wrapped around the hook.

Increasing and decreasing in the middle of the work

Increasing in single crochet. See illustration F, numbers 1 and 2.

1 Crochet a single crochet in the stitch where the increase must come.

2 Put the hook in the same stitch and crochet another single crochet in the same stitch.

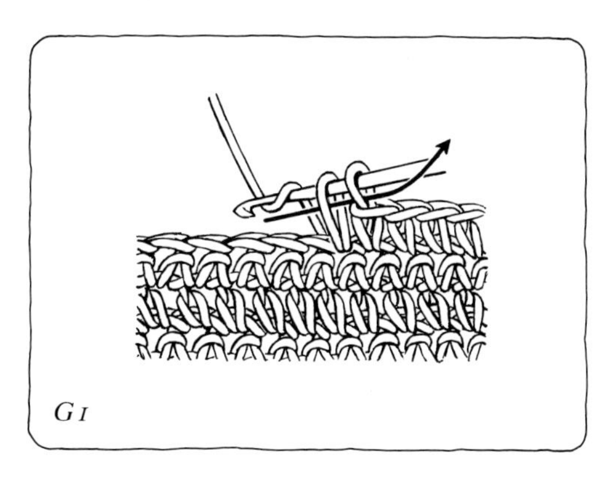

G1

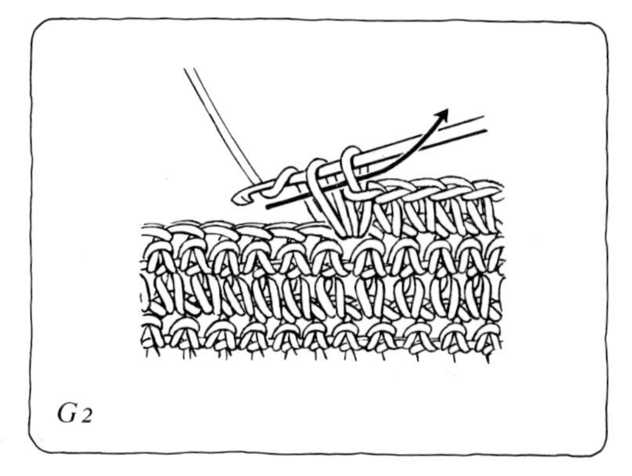

G2

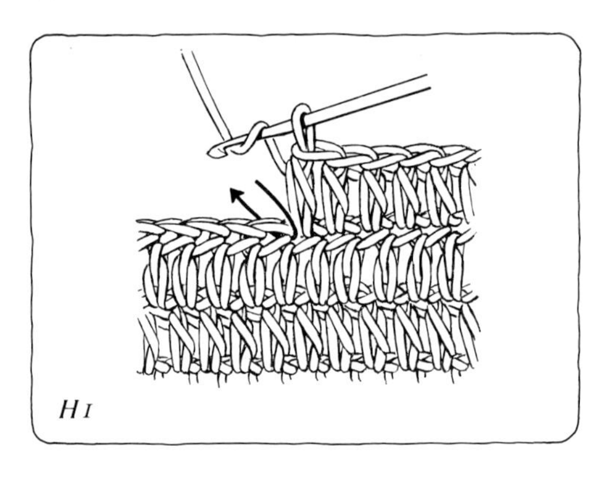

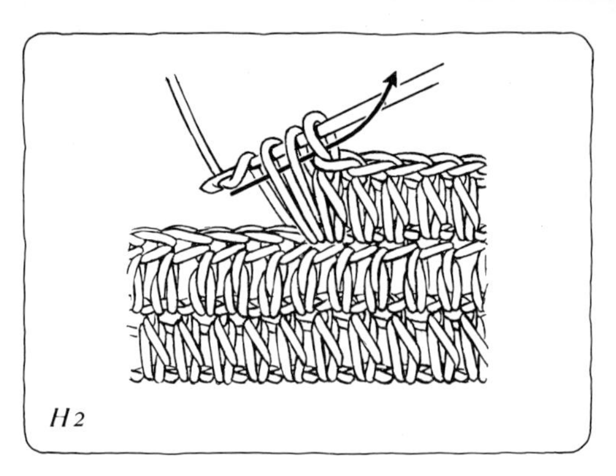

Increasing in half double crochet. See illustration H, numbers 1 and 2.

1 Crochet 1 half double crochet in the stitch where the increase must come. Wrap the yarn around the hook and put the hook into the same stitch again.
Pull up a loop and crochet a 2nd half double crochet. Increasing when working double crochet is done in the same way.

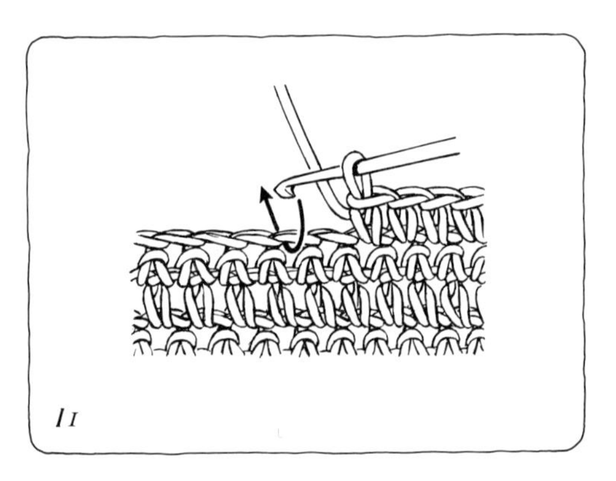

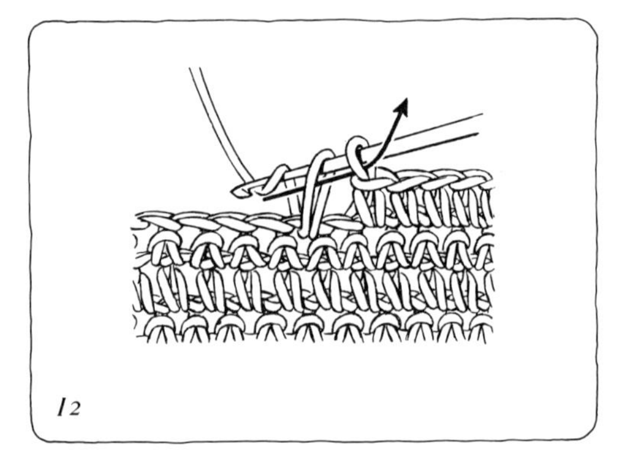

Decreasing in single crochet. See illustration I, numbers 1 and 2.

1 Skip 1 stitch at the point where the decrease will be and put the hook in the following stitch.
2 Pull a loop though and crochet in single crochet.

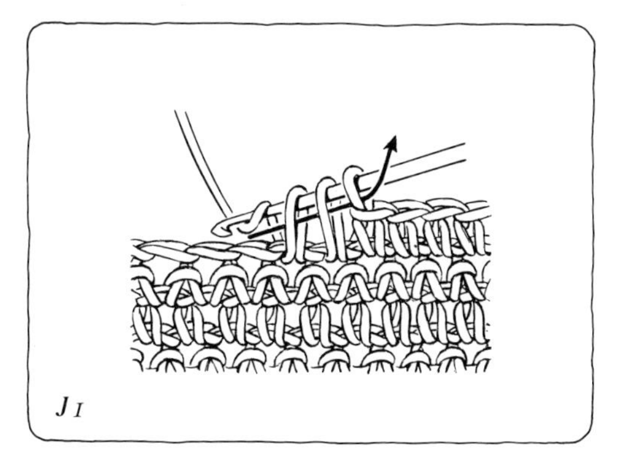

J 1

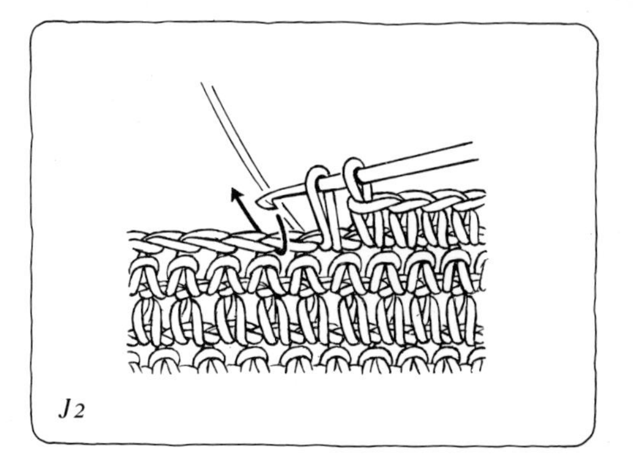

J 2

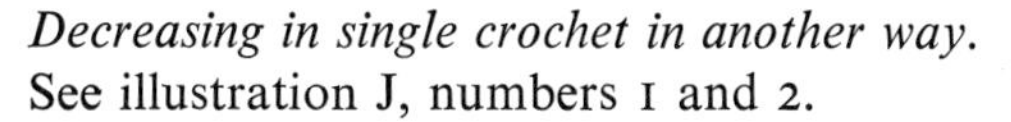

Decreasing in single crochet in another way. See illustration J, numbers 1 and 2.

The first way we described for decreasing in single crochet is not always attractive as a hole results.
To avoid this you can decrease in the following way.

1 Put the hook in the stitch at the place where you wish to decrease and pick up a loop.
2 Put the hook in the next stitch and pull a loop through that. Wrap the yarn around the hook and crochet the 3 loops on the hook off.

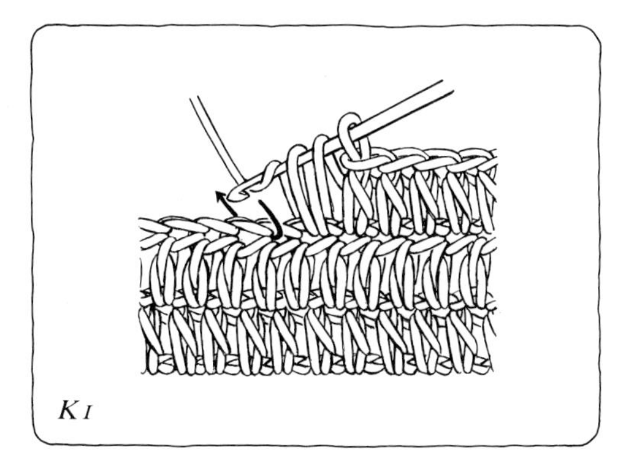

K 1

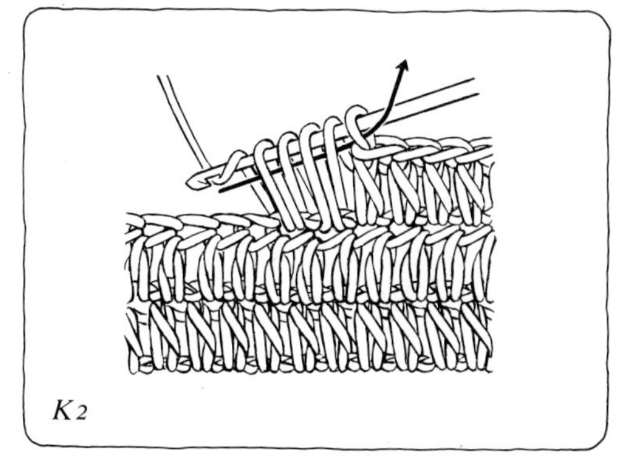

K 2

Decreasing in half double crochet. See illustration K, numbers 1 and 2.

This is the same as the method illustrated in J for decreasing in single crochet.

1 Wrap the yarn around the hook and put the hook in the stitch, pull up a loop, wrap the yarn around the hook again, and put the hook through the next stitch.
2 Pull up a loop and wrap the yarn around the hook. Pull this through the 5 loops on the hook.

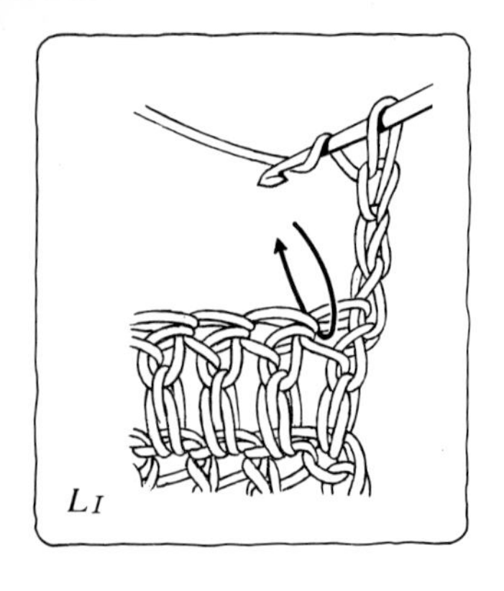

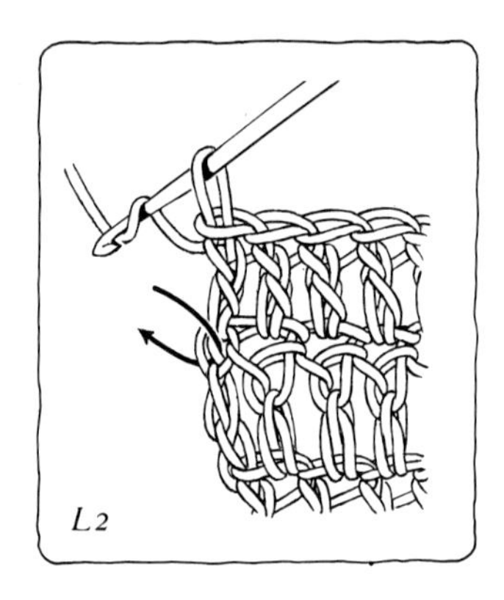

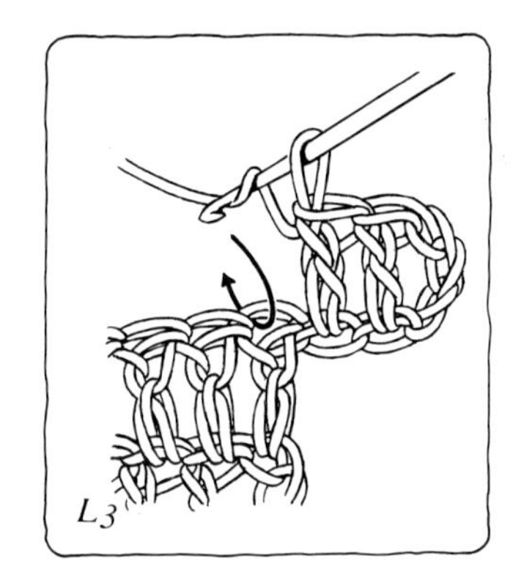

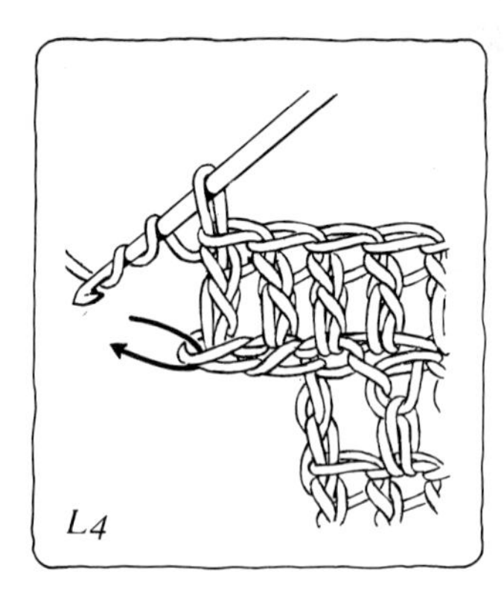

L1. Increasing 1 double crochet at the beginning of a row.
L2. Increasing 1 double crochet at the end of a row.
L3. Increasing by several double crochets at the beginning of a row, see also page 23.
L4. Increasing by several double crochets at the end of the row.

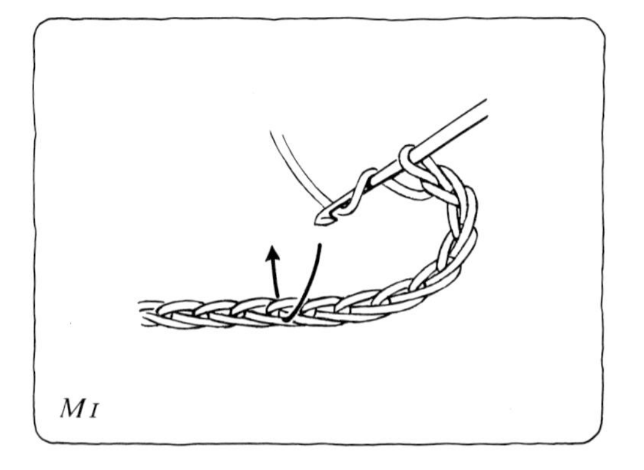

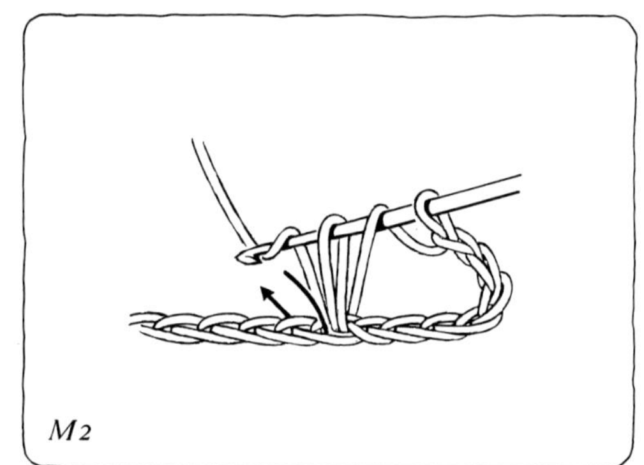

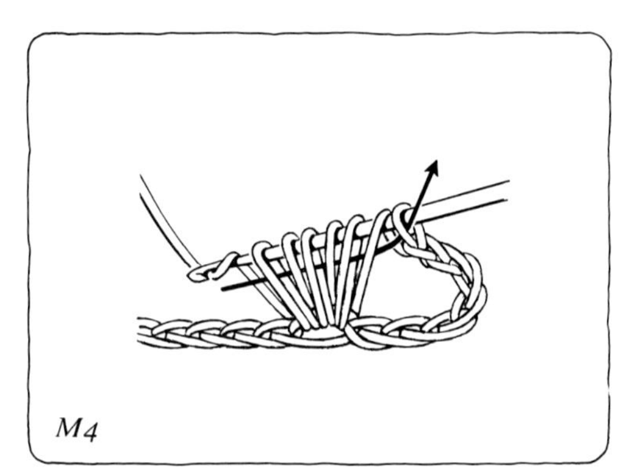

Creating texture through large loops

See illustration M, numbers 1 through 6.

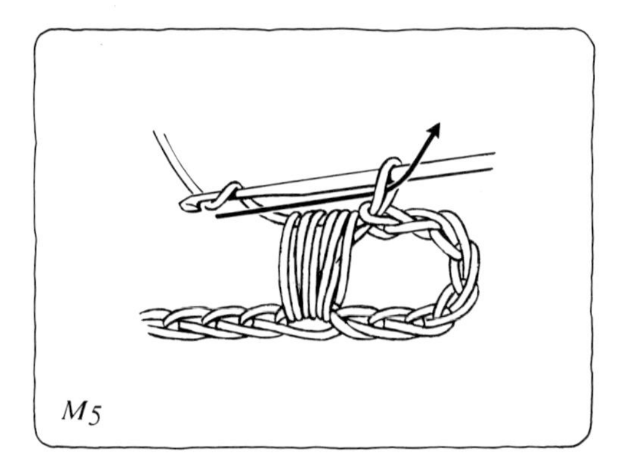

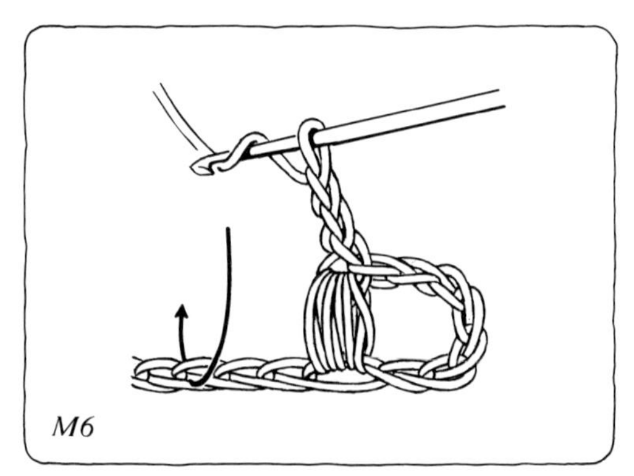

13 Some Instructions

The border on page 18

Start with the basic color at the last double crochet of the filet crochet.

1st row: crochet 4 chains for the first double crochet, * chain 1, work 1 double crochet in the next double crochet, repeat from * and end with a triple crochet in the 3rd chain from the turn. Use the next color for the last stitch (in our example this is dark green) and end the basic color.
In the following rows, when the color changes, work the last stitch with the next color and finish the other color.

2nd row: dark green, * chain 3, 1 single crochet in the following double crochet, repeat from * and end with 1 single crochet in the 4th chain of the turn. Change color.

3rd row: light green, chain 5 for the first triple crochet with 1 chain, * 1 triple crochet in the single crochet of the previous row, chain 1, repeat from * and end with 1 chain, 1 triple crochet in the last stitch.

4th row: chain 4, 1 triple crochet in the stitch under these chains, * 1 single crochet in the triple crochet, 4 triple crochets in the next triple crochet (this is a shell) repeat from * and end with 1 single crochet, 2 triple crochets in the last stitch. Change color.

5th row: basic color, chain 1, * crochet in the following single crochet: 1 triple crochet, 1 chain, 3 triple crochets, 1 chain and 1 triple crochet (this makes a large shell), then 1 chain, 1 single crochet between the 2nd and 3rd double crochet of the shell of the previous row, 1 chain, repeat from * and end with 1 single crochet in the 4th chain of the turn. Change color.

6th row: dark green, chain 4 and work 1 double crochet in the stitch under these chains, 1 single crochet in the middle double crochet of the large shell, * chain 1, crochet in the single crochet between the large shells of the previous row: 1 double crochet, 1 chain, 1 double crochet and 1 chain, then 1 single crochet in the middle double crochet of the next large shell of the previous row, repeat from * and end with 1 chain and 2 double crochets in the last stitch. Change color.

7th row: rose-red, chain 3, 2 double crochet in the stitch under these chains, 1 single crochet in the chain between the group of 2 double crochets, * 5 double crochets in the next single crochet, 1 single crochet in the stitches between the following group of 2 double crochets, repeat from * and end with 3 double crochets in the last stitch. Change color.

8th row: basic color, * chain 7, 1 single crochet in the middle double crochet of the shell, repeat from * and end with 1 single crochet in the 3rd chain of the turn.

9th and 10th rows: * chain 7, work 1 single crochet in the arch of 7 chain stitches, repeat from *. Change color after the 10th row.

11th row: light green, chain 3, 1 double crochet in the single crochet under the chain, * 1 single crochet in the chain arch, 4 double crochets in the following single crochet, repeat from * and end with 2 double crochets in the last single crochet. Change color.

12th row: dark green, 1 single crochet, * crochet in the single crochet between the shells a large shell of: 1 double crochet, 1 chain, 1 triple crochet, 1 chain, 1 double triple crochet, 1 chain, 1 triple triple crochet, 1 chain, 1 double triple crochet, 1 chain, 1 triple crochet, 1 chain, 1 double crochet, crochet then 1 single crochet in the middle of the shell of the previous row, repeat from * and end with 1 single crochet in the 3rd chain of the turn. Turn and work slip stitches to the middle of the last large shell, that is the triple triple crochet, and change color. For those of you who wish to end the border here, the instructions are: don't turn, end instead.

13th row: yellow, crochet in the middle of the large shell another large shell as in the 12th row, crochet 3 chains as the 1st double crochet in the first shell. Do not crochet single crochets between the large shells but crochet a large shell on the following triple triple crochet. Change color at the end of the row.

14th row: basic color, chain 1, * crochet on every stitch of the large shell and therefore also on the chains: 1 single crochet, 5 chains. Between every shell, therefore, there will be 5 chains. Repeat from *. Crochet the last single crochet in the 3rd chain of the turn.

15th row: chain 5, * work 1 single crochet in the single crochet above the first triple crochet of the large shell, chain 5, work 1 single crochet in the single crochet above the middle of the large shell, chain 5, 1 single crochet in the single crochet above the second triple crochet of the large shell, chain 5, 1 single crochet in the 5 arches between the shells, chain 5, repeat from * and end with 5 chains and 1 single crochet in the last stitch. Change color.

16th row: light green, chain 3, work 1 single crochet in the first arch after the turn, * chain one, work 1 double crochet in the arch before the triple crochet, chain 1, work 1 single crochet in the arch before the triple crochet, chain 1, work 1 single crochet in the following arch, chain 1, work 1 double crochet in the following arch, repeat from *. In this way double crochets are placed on the low arches and single crochets on the high arches. End with 1 double crochet in the last arch.

17th row: chain 5, work 1 triple crochet in the next stitch, * skip the chain stitch, chain 1, work 1 triple crochet in the next stitch, repeat from * and end with a triple crochet in the 2nd chain of the turn.

18th row: turn with 5 chains and crochet on each triple crochet 1 triple crochet with 1 chain, ending with a triple crochet in the 4th chain of the turn. Change color.

19th row: with dark green, chain 3 and crochet 1 double crochet in every stitch.

20th row: chain 1 and crochet in every double crochet 1 single crochet. Finish off.

The circles
Crochet the circles separately. Count the number of single crochet in the last row. For each circle you need about 11 stitches, so divide the number of stitches by 11. If the number is not exactly divisible by 11, divide the number remaining by 2. If this is 8, for example, then on each side of the border mark the 4th stitch with a thread at the 20th row.

Rozette: with rose-red crochet a chain of 6 stitches and close this with a slip stitch in the first chain into a ring.

1st row: chain 3 and crochet 19 double crochet in the ring. Close the row with a slip stitch in the 3rd chain from the beginning.

2nd row: * chain 3, crochet 1 half double crochet in the 1st chain of these 3 chains, skip 1 double crochet, work 1 single crochet in the next double crochet, repeat from * and close the row with a slip stitch in the 1st chain. Finish off. If you want the rozette to be larger, then continue to crochet double crochets making 2 double crochets in every double crochet. The small rozette has 10 points. The larger rozette will have more points (or picots). Crochet the necessary number of rozettes.

Crochet the rozettes together
With dark green crochet 5 chains or as many as in the 2nd row. Work 1 single crochet in a picot of the first round, * chain 10, 1 single crochet in a picot of the next round, repeat from * until all the rounds are joined on a chain with the bottom, ending with the same number of chains as at the beginning. On this chain first finish the border at the bottom.

The bottom edge
1st row: Chain 3, crochet in every chain 1 double crochet. Change color.

2nd row: basic color, chain 4, work 1 double crochet in the stitch under these chains, chain 1, * skip 4 double crochet, crochet in the following double crochet a shell of: 1 double crochet, 1 chain, 1 double crochet, 1 chain, 1 double crochet, 1 chain, repeat from * and end with 1 double crochet, 1 chain and 1 double crochet in the 3rd chain of the turn. Change color.

3rd row: yellow, chain 3, work 2 double crochet in the stitch under these chains, * 1 single crochet in the chain before the shell, then 3 double crochet in the chain before the middle of the shell, 3 double crochet in the chain after the middle of the shell, repeat from *. Change color.

4th row: dark green, chain 1 and crochet 1 single crochet in every stitch of the previous row. Finish off.

Joining the rozette border to the other borders
(See illustration on page 18)
Start at the beginning of the chain under the rozettes with dark green. Chain 5, then work 1 single crochet in the 3rd picot of the first circle, chain 5, work 1 single crochet in the 4th picot of the same circle, chain 5, work 1 single crochet in the 1st stitch of the 20th row, chain 5, work 1 single crochet in the 5th picot, chain 5, work 1 single crochet in the 6th picot, putting the hook into the stitch of the 20th row at the same time, with the colored yarn chain 5, 1 single crochet in the 7th picot, chain 10, then 1 single crochet in the 3rd picot of the next circle, chain 5, 1 single crochet in the chain around the circles, chain 5, 1 single crochet in the 9th picot of the first circle, chain 10, 1 single crochet in the 5th picot of the 2nd circle, chain 5, 1 single crochet in the 6th picot and in this way crochet the chain of the 20th row. Follow the illustration further. Finish as in the beginning and end.

The top of the curtain
Crochet along the starting chain of the filet crochet 1 row of double crochet, working 3 chains as the 1st double crochet. At the end of the row change color. Crochet with dark green 1 single crochet in every double crochet and finish off.

Finishing: put the curtain under a damp towel, first stretching and smoothing it, and let it dry. Sew curtain rings to the top, or crochet loops of chains and run a curtain rod through this edge.

The orange under curtains on page 21

Crochet every section separately and crochet as many sections as are needed for the width of your window. Begin at the top and crochet a chain of 75 stitches.

1st row: begin in the 4th chain from the hook and crochet 72 double crochets; the first 3 chains are the first double crochet so that the row is 73 double crochets wide.

2nd row: turn with 3 chains as the first double crochet, skip the first double crochet, work 1 double crochet in each of the following 3 double crochet so that there are 4 double crochets on the side, * chain 3, skip 2 double crochet, crochet 1 single crochet in the following double crochet, chain 3, skip 2 double crochet, crochet 1 double crochet in the next double crochet, repeat from * and end with 4 double crochet in place of 1 double crochet.

3rd row: chain 3 as the first double crochet and crochet in the following 3 double crochets 1 double crochet for the border, * chain 5, work 1 double crochet in the next double crochet, repeat from * and end with 4 double crochets; the last double crochet is worked in the 3rd chain of the turn.

4th row: work 3 chains as the first double crochet and 3 double crochets for the border, * chain 3, work 1 single crochet in the middle chain of the 5 chain arch, chain 3, work 1 double crochet in the following double crochet, repeat from * and end with 4 double crochet for the border.
Repeat the 3rd and 4th rows another 14 times or until you reach the desired length. End with a row following the 3rd row; this is the 33rd row.

34th row: chain three, work 3 double crochet for the border, * chain 3, work 1 single crochet in the middle chain of the arch of 5 chains, chain 3, work 1 double crochet in the following double crochet, repeat from * 3 times more, then, for the flower design: chain 5, work 1 double crochet in the following double crochet, 5 double crochets in the 5 chains of the arch, 1 double crochet in the double crochet, 5 chains, 1 double crochet in the double crochet and continue the row according to the pattern.

35th row: crochet in the pattern until the five chains forming the arch of the flower, crochet in this arch 1 double crochet on the first 3 chains, chain 2, skip the last 2 chains of the arch and crochet on the following 7 double crochets 1 double crochet; then work 2 chains, skip the 2 chains of the following chain arch and crochet 1 double crochet in each of the following 3 chains, work 1 double crochet in the following double crochet and continue the row in the pattern.

36th row: chain 3, work 3 double crochets for the border, chain 3, work 1 single crochet in the 3rd chain of the 5 chain arch, chain 3, work 13 double crochets (that is, on the following stitches, whether double crochet or chain stitch, work a double crochet), chain 2, work 1 double crochet in the 3rd chain of the 5 chain arch, work 2 chains, work 1 double crochet in the double crochet, chain 2, skip 2 double crochet, crochet 13 double crochet again, chain 2, skip 2 double crochet, crochet 1 double crochet in the next double crochet, chain 2, work 1 double crochet in the 3rd chain of the 5 chain arch, chain 2, skip 2 chain, double crochet 13, chain 3, work 1 single crochet in the 3rd chain of the 5 chain arch, chain 3, and work 4 double crochet for the border.

37th row: chain 3, work 3 double crochet for the border, chain 5, work 1 double crochet in the following double crochet, chain 2, skip 2 double crochet, work 16 double crochets (1 double crochet in every stitch), chain 2, skip 2 chains, work 13 double crochet, chain 2, skip 2 chains, work 16 double crochet, chain 2, skip 2 double crochet, work 1 double crochet in the next double crochet, chain 5, work 4 double crochet for the border.

38th row: chain 3, work 3 double crochet for the border, chain 3, work 1 single crochet in the 3rd chain of the 5 chain arch, chain 3, work 1 double crochet in the double crochet, chain 5, skip 2 chains and 3 double crochet; then work 16 double crochet, chain 2, skip 2 double crochet. For the heart of the flower * work 1 double crochet, chain 1, skip 1 double crochet, repeat from * twice, work 1 double crochet, chain 2, skip 2 double crochet, work 16 double crochet, chain 5, skip 3 double crochet and 2 chains, work 1 double crochet in the double crochet, chain 3, work 1 single crochet in the 3rd chain of the 5 chain arch, work 3 chains and 4 double crochet for the border.

39th row: chain 3 and work 3 double crochet for the border, chain 5, work 1 double crochet in the double crochet, chain 3, work 1 single crochet in the 3rd chain of the 5 chain arch, chain 3, work 1 double crochet in the double crochet, chain 2, skip 2 double crochet, work 13 double crochet, chain 2, then for the center * work 1 double crochet, chain 1, repeat from * twice, work 1 double crochet, chain 2, skip 2 chain, work 13 double crochet and finish the row as before the first 13 double crochet, that is, chain 2, skip 2 double crochet, work 1 double crochet in the following double crochet and so forth.

40th row: chain 3 and work 3 double crochet for the border, chain 3, work 1 single crochet in the 3rd chain, chain 3, work 1 double crochet in the double crochet, chain 5, work 1 double crochet in the double crochet, chain 2, skip 2 chains, work 1 double crochet in the 1st double crochet of the group of 13 double crochet, chain 2, skip 2 double crochet, work 7 double crochet, chain 2, skip 2 double crochet, work 1 double crochet, chain 2, skip 2 chains, make the center of the pattern as in the previous row, work 1 double crochet, chain 2, work 1 double crochet in the next double crochet, chain 2, skip 2 double crochet, work 7 double crochet and finish the row as for the 7 double crochet at the beginning.

41st row: chain 3 and work 3 double crochet for the border, chain 5, work 1 double crochet in the double crochet, chain 3, work 1 single crochet in the 3rd chain, chain 3, work 1 double crochet in the double crochet, chain 5, skip 2 chain, 1 double crochet, and the next 2 chain, work 7 double crochet above the 7 double crochet of the previous row, crochet chains over chains and double crochets over double crochets for the center, then work 7 double crochet again and end the row as for the first 7 double crochet.

42nd row: chain 3 and work 3 double crochet for the border, chain 3, work 1 single crochet in the 3rd chain, chain 3, work 1 double crochet in the double crochet, chain 5, work 1 double crochet in the double crochet, chain 2, work 1 double crochet in the 3rd chain of the 5 chain arch, chain 2, work 1 double crochet in the double crochet, chain 2, skip 2 double crochet, work 4 double crochet, work the center as previously, then crochet 4 double crochet, chain 2, skip 2 double crochet, work 1 double crochet in the last double crochet, chain 2, work 1 double crochet in the 3rd chain of the 5 chain arch, chain 2, work 1 double crochet in the double crochet and work the rest of the row as the beginning.

43rd row: chain 3 and work 3 double crochet for the border, chain 5, work 1 double crochet in the double crochet, chain 3, work 1 single crochet in the 3rd chain, chain 3, work 7 double crochet, chain 2, skip 2 chain and crochet in each of the following 4 double crochet 1 double crochet, crochet the center – chains above chains and double crochet above double crochet – and finish the row in reverse, that is, after the center work 4 double crochet, 2 chains, 7 double crochet and so forth.

44th row: chain 3 and work 3 double crochet for the border, chain 3, work 1 single crochet in the 3rd chain, chain 3, work 1 double crochet in the double crochet, chain 5, work 1 double crochet in the double crochet, chain 2, skip 2 double crochet, work 13 double crochet, then for the center work 2 chains, work 1 double crochet in the double crochet, chain 1, work 1 double crochet, chain 1, work 1 double crochet, chain 1, work 1 double crochet, chain 2, skip 2 chains, work 13 double crochet and finish the row in reverse.

45th row: chain 3 and work 3 double crochet for the border, chain 5, work 1 double crochet in the double crochet, chain 3, work 1 single crochet in the 3rd chain, chain 3, work 1 double crochet in the double crochet, continue to work as in the previous row, that is, chains over chains and double crochet over double crochet, ending the row in the pattern as at the beginning.

46th row: chain 3 and work 3 double crochet for the border, chain 5, work 1 double crochet in the double crochet, chain 3, work 1 single crochet in the 3rd chain, chain 3, work 1 double crochet in the double crochet, work as in the previous row, that is, chains over chains and double crochet over double crochet, ending the row in the pattern as at the beginning of the row.

46th row: chain 3 and work 3 double crochet for the crochet border, chain 3, work 1 single crochet in the 3rd chain, chain 3, work 1 double crochet, chain 5, work 1 double crochet, chain 2, work 1 double crochet on the next double crochet, chain 2, skip 2 double crochet, chain 1, work 1 double crochet in the double crochet, chain 1, work 1 double crochet in the double crochet, chain 1, work 13 double crochet and finish the row in reverse.

47th row: chain 3 and work 3 double crochet for the border, chain 5, work 1 double crochet in the double crochet, chain 3, work 1 single crochet in the 3rd chain, chain 3, work 1 double crochet, chain 5, skip 2 chains, 1 double crochet, and 2 chains, work 1 double crochet in the next double crochet, chain 2, skip 2 double crochet, crochet 25 double crochet and end the row in reverse.

48th row: chain 3 and work 3 double crochet for the border, chain 3, work 1 single crochet in the 3rd chain, chain 3, work 1 double crochet in the double crochet, chain 5, work 1 double crochet in the double crochet, chain 3, work 1 single crochet in the 3rd chain, chain 3, work 1 double crochet in the double crochet, chain 2 three times, skip 2 stitches, work 1 double crochet. Work 12 double crochet so that there are 13 double crochet in the middle then again work 2 chains three times, skip 2 stitches, work 1 double crochet, and end the row in reverse.

49th row: chain 3 and work 3 double crochet for the border, chain 5, work 1 double crochet in the double crochet, chain 3, work 1 single crochet in the 2rd chain, chain 3, work 1 double crochet, chain 5, work 1 double crochet, work 2 chains three times, work 1 double crochet, work 2 chains, skip 2 double crochet, work 7 double crochet, chain 2, skip 2 double crochet, work 1 double crochet and finish the row in reverse.

50th row: chain 3 and work 3 double crochet for the border, chain 3, work 1 single crochet in the 3rd chain, chain 3, work 1 double crochet, chain 5, work 10 double crochet, chain 2 seven times, work 1 double crochet, chain 2, work 10 double crochet and finish the row in reverse.

51st row: chain 3 and work 3 double crochet for the border, chain 5, work 1 double crochet, chain 3, work 1 single crochet in the 3rd chain, chain 3, work 1 double crochet, chain 2, skip 2 double crochet, work 10 double crochet, chain 2, work 1 double crochet 5 times, chain 2, work 10 double crochet and continue the row in reverse.

52nd row: chain 3 and work 3 double crochet for the border, chain 3, work 1 single crochet in the 3rd chain, chain 3, work 1 double crochet, chain 2, work 1 double crochet in the following double crochet, chain 2, skip 2 double crochet, work 10 double crochet, chain 2, work 1 double crochet 3 times, chain 2, then work 10 double crochet and finish the row in reverse.

53rd row: chain 3 and work 3 double crochet for the border, chain 5, work 1 double crochet, chain 3, work 1 single crochet in the 3rd chain, chain 3, work 1 double crochet, chain 5, skip 2 double crochet, work 10 double crochet, chain 2, work 1 double crochet, chain 2, work 10 double crochet and finish the row in reverse.

54th row: this row starts the decreasing. Work slip stitches until the 4th double crochet, chain 2 and work 3 double crochet in the first 3 chains of the 5 chain arch, chain 2, work 1 double crochet in the next double crochet, chain 5, work 1 double crochet, chain 3, work 1 single crochet in the 3rd chain, chain 3, work 1 double crochet, chain 5, skip 2 chains and 3 double crochet, work 19 double crochet, chain 5, skip 3 double crochet and 2 chain, work 1 double crochet, chain 3, work 1 single crochet in the 3rd chain, chain 3, work 1 double crochet, chain 5, work 1 double crochet, chain 2, skip 2 chain of the 5 chain arch, crochet 1 double crochet in each of the last 3 chains of this arch, work 1 double crochet in the 1st double crochet and turn.

55th row: work slip stitches until the 4th double crochet of the border, work 3 chains and 3 double crochet for the border in the 2 chains and the double crochet, then work 2 chains, work 1 double crochet in the 3rd chain, chain 2 and work 1 double crochet in the next double crochet, chain 5, work 1 double crochet, chain 3, work 1 single crochet in the 3rd chain, chain 3, work 1 double crochet, chain 2, skip 2 double crochet, work 13 double crochet, chain 2, skip 2 double crochet, work 1 double crochet, chain 3, work 1 single crochet in the 3rd chain, chain 3, work 1 double crochet, chain 5, work 1 double crochet, chain 2, work 1 double crochet in the 3rd chain, chain 2, work 1 double crochet and 2 double crochet in the first 2 chains, work 1 double crochet in the double crochet and turn.

56th row: work slip stitches until the 4th double crochet, chain 3 and work 3 double crochet for the border in the first 2 chains and the following double crochet, chain 2, work 1 double crochet in the double crochet, chain 3, work 1 single crochet in the 3rd chain, chain 3, work 1 double crochet, chain 5, work 1 double crochet, chain 2, work 1 double crochet in the first double crochet, chain 2, skip 2 double crochet, work 7 double crochet, chain 2, skip 2 double crochet, work 1 double crochet in the last double crochet, chain 2, work 1 double crochet, chain 5, work 1 double crochet, chain 3, work 1 single crochet in the 3rd chain, chain 3, work 1 double crochet, chain 2, work 1 double crochet, work 1 double crochet in each of the following 2 chains, work 1 double crochet in the 1st double crochet and turn.

57th row: chain 3 and work 3 double crochet for the border, chain 2, work 1 double crochet, chain 5, work 1 double crochet, chain 3, work 1 single crochet in the 3rd chain, chain 3, work 1 double crochet, chain 5, skip 2 chain, 1 double crochet, and 2 chain, work 7 double crochet, chain 5, and finish the row in reverse. There is no decreasing in this row.

58th row: work slip stitches until the 4th double crochet of the border, crochet 3 chains and 3 double crochet as in the 56th row, chain 2, work 1 double crochet in the 3rd chain, chain 3, work 1 double crochet, chain 5, work 1 double crochet, chain 3, work 1 single crochet in the 3rd chain, chain 3, work 7 double crochet, chain 3, work 1 single crochet in the 3rd chain, chain 3, work 1 double crochet, chain 5, work 1 double crochet, chain 2, work 1 double crochet in the 3rd chain, chain 2, work 1 double crochet, work 2 double crochet on the 2 chain and 1 double crochet on the 1st double crochet and turn.

59th row: work slip stitches until the 4th double crochet of the border, chain 3, work 3 double crochet, chain 2, work 1 double crochet, chain 2 and skip 2 chain, crochet 1 double crochet on each of the following 3 chains, work 1 double crochet on the double crochet, chain 5, work 7 double crochet, chain 5, work 1 double crochet, crochet 1 double crochet in each of the 3 first chains, chain 2, work 1 double crochet in the double crochet, chain 2, work 1 double crochet in the double crochet, work 2 double crochet in the chain and 1 double crochet in the double crochet and turn.

60th row: chain 3 and work 3 double crochet for the border, chain 2, work 1 double crochet, chain 2, work 1 double crochet in the next double crochet, chain 2, skip 2 double crochet, work 1 double crochet in the next double crochet, work 1 double crochet in each of the following first 3 chains, chain 2, skip 2 chains, work 7 double crochet, chain 2, skip 2 chain and work 1 double crochet in each of the following 3 chains, work 1 double crochet in the double crochet, chain 2, skip 2 double crochet, work 1 double crochet in the following double crochet, chain 2, work 1 double crochet, chain 2 and work 4 double crochet for the border.

61st row: work slip stitches until the 4th double crochet of the border, chain 3 and work 3 double crochet for the border, * chain 5, skip 5 stitches, work 1 double crochet, repeat from * 4 times, end with 2 double crochet in the chains and 1 double crochet in the double crochet and turn.

62nd row: work slip stitches until the 4th double crochet, chain 3, and crochet 30 double crochet – 1 double crochet in every stitch. Finish off.
Crochet the number of sections you need for the width of the window.

Decorative border: begin on the right side and put the hook in between the 1st and 2nd double crochet. Crochet 3 chains and 1 double crochet in the same stitch, chain 6, work 1 single crochet in the 1st chain of these 6 (picot) and 2 double crochet in the same stitch, * skip 6 double crochet, crochet in the space in between: 2 double crochet, 1 picot and 2 double crochet, repeat from * 11 more times, skipping only 5 double crochet the last time; continue to crochet along the long side as follows: * 1 picot, skip 1 row, crochet 3 double crochet in the 3 chains of the turn of the following row, repeat from * 24 times, then work 1 picot; work on the slanting bottom: * 2 double crochet, 1 picot, and 2 double crochet in the 'small corner', repeat from * 6 times; crochet on the right bottom 2 double crochet, 1 picot, and 2 double crochet in the next space, that is between the first 2 double crochet, * skip 6 double crochet and work in the following space 2 double crochet, 1 picot, and 2 double crochet, repeat from * 4 times; skip 5 double crochet the last time. Crochet along the other sides in the same way and close the row with a slip stitch in the first chain. Finish off.
Crochet the strips to each other. To do this place 2 strips against each other with the right sides up. Put the hook in the first picot and crochet 3 chain, work 1 single crochet in the picot of the 2nd strip corresponding to the first, work 3 chain, work 1 single crochet in the 2nd picot of the 1st strip, chain 3 and work 1 single crochet in the 2nd picot of the 2nd strip with 3 chains in between.

Finishing: put all sections under a damp towel and let this dry. Sew rings along the top section, 2 for each strip, or sew more small rings on.

CREDITS

author and editor	Rite van der Klip
translator	Irene Cumming Kleeberg
samples	Scheepjeswol, Veenendaal
cover sample	M. M. Glaser-van Orden
title page illustration	José de Wolff
photography	Ed Suister
design	Chris van Egmond
typesetting	Internationaal Zetcentrum b.v., Wormerveer
printing	Drukkerij Meijer Wormerveer b.v.
binding	Callenbach n.v., Nijkerk
production	Ideeboek b.v., Amsterdam

Published in cooperation with Scheepjeswol,
Veenendaal, The Netherlands